JING

BREAD
and Roses

BREAD

and Roses

Arts, Culture
and Lifelong
Learning

JANE THOMPSON

Published by the National Institute of
Adult Continuing Education (England and Wales)

21 De Montfort Street
Leicester LEl 7GE
Company registration no. 2603322
Charity registration no. 1002775

First published 2002

niace
promoting adult learning

NIACE has a broad remit to promote lifelong learning opportunities for
adults. NIACE works to develop increased participation in education and
training, particularly for those who do not have easy access because of
barriers of class, gender, age, race, language and culture, learning difficulties
and disabilities, or insufficient financial resources.

www.niace.org.uk

Cataloguing in Publication Data
A CIP record of this title is available from the British Library

Designed and typeset by Lee Robinson / Ad Lib Design, London N19
Printed in Great Britain by Hobbs the Printers Ltd, Hampshire

Cover photos: Richard Olivier, Foundation for Community Dance,
               1st Framework
Photo overleaf: Ariel from *The Tempest* / Lawrence Burns –
               1st Framework

ISBN: 1 86201 134 6

CONTENTS

ACKNOWLEDGEMENTS

My thanks to Sheila Carlton, Veronica McGivney, Judith Summers, Alan Tuckett and Sylvia Vance for their insightful comments on the first draft of *Bread and Roses*.

INTRODUCTION

T he imagery of bread and roses has been a recurring theme through-out the recent history of popular education. It was the slogan used by women garment workers in New York in 1908 when they marched after the death of 128 women in a factory tenement fire. Four years later the slogan appeared on the banner of women textile workers on strike in Lawrence, Massachusetts – WE WANT BREAD AND WE WANT ROSES TOO. They were demanding equal pay for equal work and an end to discrimination against foreign-born workers. The strike involved 22,000 men women and children from 27 different ethnic groups, speaking many different languages. After ten weeks the strikers won important concessions from the woollen companies, not only for themselves but also for 250,000 textile workers throughout New England.

This campaign song, written by James Oppenheim to music by Martha Coleman, was inspired by their resilience and achievement:

As we go marching, marching in the beauty of the day,
A million darkened kitchens, a thousand mill lofts grey,
Are touched with all the radiance that a sudden sun discloses,
For the people hear us singing: "Bread and roses! Bread and roses!"

As we go marching, marching, we battle too for men,
For they are women's children, and we mother them again.
Our lives shall not be sweated from birth until life closes;
Hearts starve as well as bodies; give us bread, but give us roses!

As we go marching, marching, unnumbered women dead
Go crying through our singing their ancient cry for bread.
Small art and love and beauty their drudging spirits knew.
Yes, it is bread we fight for – but we fight for roses, too!

As we come marching, marching, we bring the greater days.
The rising of the women means the rising of the race.
No more the drudge and idler – ten that toil where one reposes,
But a sharing of life's glories: Bread and roses! Bread and roses!
Our lives shall not be sweated from birth until life closes;
Hearts starve as well as bodies; give us bread, but give us roses.

It is perhaps not surprising that this historical struggle, led by not very powerful and poorly paid immigrant women, on behalf of fellow textile workers, should – in another country at another time – still make us think about the relationship between work and discrimination, material and spiritual sustenance, cultural difference and common purpose, and how all of these relate to education, arts and culture. Nearly 90 years later, in his speech to the Royal Society of Arts, the then Secretary of State, Chris Smith, quoted from Oppenheim's tribute to the women strikers. In recognising that 'it is bread we fight for but we fight for roses too' Smith concluded that the women's rallying cry should serve as a reminder to any government that 'the fine things of life should be part of the struggle for better conditions for all', and added, 'we won't ignore it'[1]

There can be few who would disagree with the ideal, that in the fourth richest economy in the world – in what is widely held to be a just and democratic society – its citizens should expect a reasonable standard of iving; the right to a decent job; a political system which depends upon their engaged participation in ways that directly relate to their lives; and a social system which has equality, social justice and respect for others at its heart. These are critical issues for all citizens. They are the professional business of politicians, economists and social scientists. But they also pose important questions for education, arts and cultural workers. To what extent does our work as policy-makers, providers, practitioners, and volunteers contribute to advancing this ideal of a more equitable and more creative society? It is certain that our contribution will count one way or the other. Do we contribute to the solution? Or do we exacerbate the problem?

We live in a political climate in which the government of the day has made education and social inclusion two of its principal concerns. It has made it clear that lifelong learning has an important part to play in both increasing national and individual prosperity and encouraging social cohesion. It has determined to reduce poverty, combat social exclusion and promote active citizenship. It has recognised that arts and culture have an important contribution to make to these ambitions, in ways that more formal education and social policy approaches struggle to achieve.

These are all aspirations which are music to the ears of social reformers and radicals, those who welcome the realisation of a more equal, a more tolerant and a more politically engaged society. They certainly provide opportunities to further these ideals. But they also require imaginative, energetic and concerted action. Translating policy rhetoric into the kinds of reality that will engage the commitment of practitioners and arouse the enthusiasm of participants represents a huge challenge.

In this context, neither education nor culture are neutral. What counts as knowledge and art – how we create and practise, select and interpret, and distribute it, and for what purposes – reflects historic, political, cultural and gendered decisions, made in social situations, in which some people are more powerful than others, both socially and institutionally. Both knowledge and art are social constructs. Some of what is created goes with the grain of dominant values and ideas. Some of it challenges and calls into question what is widely taken for granted. The dynamic, the dialectic, the contest and the negotiation all serve to constitute and re-constitute both of them through human interaction. Alternatives are created. Different kinds make perfect sense in different contexts. Some kinds have more status than others, usually depending on the status of those who create and give value to them.

What counts as knowledge and art is closely related to what counts as education and culture. It is precisely because they are not finite or neutral that education and culture are also not neutral. They can be used to free people or to constrain them, to empower them or to weaken them, to include or exclude them. For these and other reasons, both education and culture are central to the democratic life of any society. They are worth fighting for. They can act to reinforce the *status quo* and conform people to the logic of the present system. Or they can be a powerful tonic for the imagination and a necessary resource for progressive social change.

At the same time, educational and cultural organisations are not particularly radical or democratic social institutions. Many have every interest in not changing, or not changing any more than they have to. Twenty years (at least) of market economics, new managerialism, competitive individualism and political cynicism have, in a variety ways, added to existing social inequalities and reduced the will to challenge them.

But since New Labour came to power, the possibility of expanding education and the arts and engaging more people in their benefits has returned to the political agenda in ways that must be welcomed. Speaking just a few days after the 1997 election Chris Smith said, 'the arts are for everyone. Things of quality must be available to the many, not just the few. Cultural activity is not some elitist exercise that takes place in reverential temples aimed at the predilections of the *cognoscenti*. The opportunity to create and to enjoy must be fostered for all'[2].

However, there are dangers lurking in the arrangements that are now being made to secure these aspirations. Five years down the line, we have learned the appropriate language to use when we are arguing for resources, about the targets we have to meet, how to monitor and measure and benchmark what we do. Possibly this makes a difference. There are always individuals ready to claim that education or art has changed their lives. But changing the lives of whole communities of people, especially communities of excluded and relatively powerless people, is something which requires a different kind of collaboration and a different quality of commitment. Making educational and cultural institutions more accountable to those who fund them may modernise and improve the quality of the services they provide, but this is not necessarily the same as – or has anything to do with – creating a more socially just, culturally enriching or actively democratic society. Not everything that is worth doing is easily measured. In the same way, not everything that is easily measured is worth worrying about. According to Richard Noble, 'there is a real danger that top-down bureaucratic leadership will achieve the opposite of what it intends. Instead of inspiring a lasting and substantial diversity that truly reflects the reality of Britain, it could promote banal and patronising programming that will alienate the public and artists alike'[3].

ARTS AND CULTURE FOR THE PEOPLE?

On 1 December 2001 the decision to drop entrance charges to national museums resulted in an almost immediate increase in visitor numbers the following weekend. According to *The Times*, attractions such as the Science Museum and the Natural History Museum more than doubled their visitor numbers, despite the Natural History Museum being an earlier critic of the reform, on the grounds that people only really appreciate that for which they have to pay. The following Sunday, the Museum of London reported a five-fold increase in visitor numbers. The preliminary evidence suggests something of the same phenomenon that has made a huge popular success of Tate Modern – especially when what is on offer is beautifully and accessibly displayed and not boring.

It is also in line with continental European experience, suggesting that government investment in culture – especially over the long-term – is likely to increase access and participation. In Finland, for example, generous investment in the cultural infrastructure in the 1980s has provided one of the best library networks in the world and one of the highest ratios of museums to people – around 900 museums in a population less than the size of London. In Sweden, making a priority of opportunities for everyone to take part as both consumers and creators of culture, supported by high government spending, means that attendance has been growing steadily over the last 25 years with about half the population actually taking part in some form of artistic activity.

High spending does not necessarily guarantee participation, however. France spends around one per cent of its state budget on the cultural sector and has an active cultural education policy. Whilst this means that almost half the French population over the age of 15 is engaged in some form of cultural activity and that attendance at arts facilities, museums and galleries have all increased – including a highly significant rise in library membership – a study in the late 1990s revealed that more than a quarter of the French population had not read a single book in the previous 12 months and that literacy remains a huge issue.

It could be that not everyone enjoys the arts. And we should not, even in the interests of social inclusion, be determined to frog-march reluctant conscripts into libraries or museums and galleries because the powers-that-be or those-in-the-know imagine it will be good for them. In the event, we scarcely know what people would do if they had a real choice because what counts as art has never been genuinely available to everyone. Not so long ago in Britain (and still so in many respects) the arts were self-consciously elitist and proudly exclusive. There was an "us" (educated, cultured, superior) and a "them" (everyone else). More recently, the winds of change have been blowing through the cultural establishment. Whilst a few influential voices still argue the opposite, the arts are increasingly supposed to be both culturally democratic and accessible to all, not least because their funding depends upon it. One of the major aims of the Arts Council, for instance, is to 'promote access, education and excellence in the arts through partnership' with priorities that include bringing the arts to a wider audience.

If it is true that more people get involved in the arts as soon as they become more physically, culturally and financially accessible – this suggests a complementary role for education. The prospects are encouraging. According to John Crace, ordinary people are now more confident when it comes to engaging with works of art that might previously have been considered dull or incomprehensible. He cites as an example Martin Creed's Turner Prize-winning installation of *Lights Going On and Off* at Tate Britain[4]. After receiving his cheque for £20,000, Creed commented, 'It's not for me to explain it. People can make of it what they like'. The BBC's arts correspondent, Rosie Millard, reminding us of Creed's other work which includes a scrunched-up ball of paper and a lump of blue-tack, said, 'It's very joyful and something which people can easily re-create in their own homes'. The museum's curator talked rather more seriously about 'the movement towards the dematerialisation of art since the sixties'. Most of the general public, it seems, concluded that an empty room with a light flicking on and off was a pretentious conceit. But what matters was that although there were many who hated it, they tried to respond to it critically, as a work of art. Crace attributes this heightened confidence not to education but to the ways in which culture is now seen as being more varied and legitimate and because television has been able to entertain and enlighten people about the classics, history, natural history and music, for example, in ways that – at their best – are immensely accessible and informative.

Whilst New Labour clearly recognises that the creative industries provide thousands of jobs and are worth billions of pounds a year to the British economy, and that greater access to the arts might help to reduce crime and long-term unemployment, boost people's health and improve their qualifications, this has not yet led to the kinds of dedicated educational policies that are common in France and Scandinavia. In schools it can seem as though the reverse is true. As a result of funding shortages, literacy and numeracy imperatives, the standards debate and school league tables, many – so-called 'bog standard' – schools have largely given up on general music teaching and arts and crafts because, in such a climate, subjects that aren't tested are not seen as a priority. In the process 'a generation of schoolchildren have had their access both to practical artistic experience and to a wider appreciation of aesthetics severely compromised'[5].

In terms of adult education, present-day enthusiasts for lifelong learning still have to argue passionately in favour of art for art's sake because of increasing pressures to deliver job skills and easy-to-measure social benefits. So long as arts, crafts and music courses are viewed as rather self-indulgent leisure pursuits, associated with more affluent students who can afford to pay for them – or in a different context, remedial subjects for adults with social problems or learning difficulties – then assumptions which serve to reinforce both the class nature of participation in cultural activities as well as derogatory connotations about art as therapy go unchallenged.

Where many schools have given up, and adult education struggles to restore some of its earlier convictions, arts organisations, museums, galleries and the media are trying to step in. What is at issue, however, is the social diversity of those who currently enjoy, and who are increasing their engagement with, arts and culture. Are they the same sort of people who would have attended arts events in the past and are now enjoying them more often and in different ways? Or are they people from social groups which were previously excluded from what arts and culture have to offer, and who are now being drawn in for the first time?

A related issue when it comes to access and government funding – in the context of an audit culture – is that the concern for head-counting can become more important than what is being offered. Targeting policies can contribute to ticking-off and adding in relevant groups, for reasons of political and funding expediencies, as a way of avoiding more fundamental change. Education becomes reduced to a marketing strategy. When the attempt is made to accommodate the excluded in a process of inclusion, the accommodation can lead to assimilation. Sometimes, what is different becomes exoticised as a kind of inoculation against the social implications of difference.

It is certain that the Department of Culture, Media and Sport (DCMS) is committed to increasing access to the arts and to contributing to social inclusion. Unlike some European equivalents, this is not a big department with a big budget. But the signs are that it is trying to put its money where its mouth is. It has found the cash to end admission charges at national museums, as we have seen, and in the words of its current arts minister, Tessa Blackstone, it wants 'minimum bureaucracy, maximum money'.

In a former life Baroness Blackstone was the Master of Birkbeck College and when in Government the Minister for Lifelong Learning. We should expect her to champion education and not be surprised when we hear that she is in favour of ordinary people becoming increasingly involved in doing art rather than simply looking at it. What is less clear is whether she is in favour of ordinary people developing and cultivating artistic passions as of right, in the context of cultural democracy, or because this could help reduce the demands on social and healthcare budgets. Whilst there is considerable evidence to support the conviction that participation in arts, culture and lifelong learning makes a qualitative difference to people's day-to-day existence, this is not the main reason why they should be supported. Creating more opportunities for wider participation in arts, culture and lifelong learning must not be seen as an alternative to improved social and public services for those who are most dependent on them.

The purpose of this publication is to address some of these issues and to explore the links between arts, culture and lifelong learning, especially in relation to social exclusion. I shall argue in support of policies and practices that recognise the importance to ordinary people of having bread and roses. I shall assume that earning a living ought not to be calculated simply in terms of utilitarian skills or private profit and that there is more to life than paid labour. Article 27 of the Universal Declaration of Human Rights, for example, states that 'everyone has the right freely to participate in the cultural life of the community, to enjoy the arts and to share in scientific advancement and its benefits'. I shall assume that the full entitlements of citizenship in a democratic society ought to enhance the quality of people's lives and engage with their imagination and creativity, as well as make space for active participation in civil society.

In the light of these assumptions, I will look briefly at what we mean by art and culture and how the provision of lifelong learning through the arts is responding to the creation of a learning society. I shall identify some of the

concerns that inform government policies in relation to social exclusion and look at the recommendations being made to address them. I will consider which developments should be supported and where changes are necessary. By way of inspiration, I shall include some illustrations of the many terrific activities and achievements I have discovered along the way which are making a positive difference to people's lives.

---

[1] C Smith, Secretary of State for Culture, Media and Sport Lecture at the RSA London 22 July 1999

[2] C Smith, speech to the Annual Dinner of the Royal Academy, London 22 May 1997

[3] R Noble 'Accessibility for All. Freedom for the Few' in *Art for All? Their Policies and Our Culture* (2000) ed Mark Wallinger and Mary Warnock, London: Peer

[4] J Crace (2001) 'Getting the Knowledge' in *Arts for All?, The Guardian*, 10 December 2001

[5] *ibid*

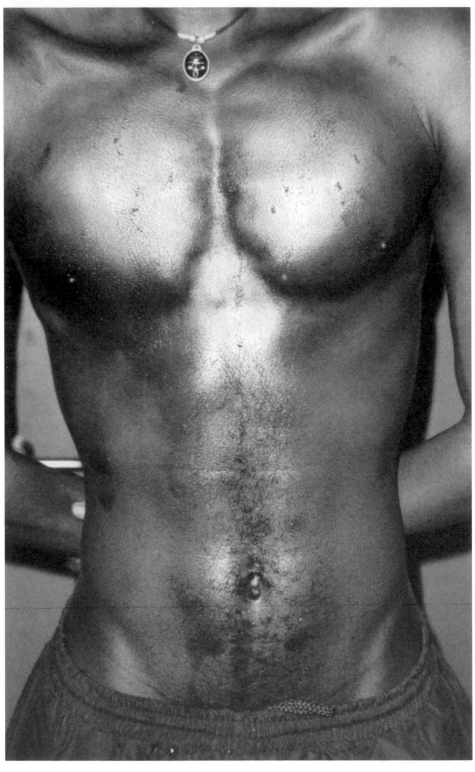

STUDIES OF
BODY BY KA▮
TAKEN FROM
SIXTY TONG▮
BEDFORD PR▮
INVOLVING Y▮
PEOPLE.

THE BEDFORD F▮
BEDFORD MUSE▮
CECIL HIGGINS A▮

Arts, Culture
and
Education

1
ARTS AND CULTURE

Culture is a complicated word with a range of meanings. In the course of this book I shall use the term in both of two ways. In an anthropological sense, culture is used to refer to the beliefs and values – in fact, the whole way of life – of a society or social group. Defined like this, the social construction of culture comes from growing up with others in a social context, in a society that shares a history and is actively building a future. It involves social actors making sense of their feelings and includes the shaping of minds, the learning of new skills, the forming and shifting of relationships, and the emergence of different kinds of language and ideas. It acts to identify a heritage; to recognise specific traditions; to influence appearance and dress; to create organisations, artifacts and icons; and to inform gender identity and behaviour.

The term "culture" is also used in an artistic sense to refer to what are conventionally thought of as the arts. In contemporary Britain this includes the arts of music, song and dance; literature including drama and poetry; painting and sculpture; television, video, photography and film.

The existence, reproduction and appreciation of what counts as artistic culture depends on social values and social practices, concerned with selecting, identifying and creating art; on institutions such as art galleries and arts centres, museums, theatres, libraries and dance companies; and on organisations such as the Arts Council. It also relies on the acquisition of certain kinds of knowledge, involving some kind of educational experience, most frequently but not always in cultural and educational institutions. In this sense, the taste for what constitutes the arts is not only experienced but also learned.

In many respects, conventional wisdom about the arts produces categories that create exclusion rather than invite inclusion. Those who do not appreciate or participate are often seen, and may sometimes see themselves, as ignorant, insensitive or lacking in the finer sensibilities of those who do. Distinctions are made between high culture and mass culture, between the elite tradition which views great art as the best that has been thought and said and the popular tradition which seeks to democratise the arts and make them more a part of shared experience.

CULTURE AND EVERYDAY LIFE

Writing about culture and adult education, Raymond Williams was reluctant to distinguish some things as art and then separate them, as if with a park wall, from ordinary people and ordinary work. 'Our specialisms will be finer,' he said, 'if they come from a common culture, rather than being a distinction from it'[6]. He cherished the idea of a shared culture, rooted in the lived experience of everyday life and created with the involvement – albeit in different ways – of everyone. For Williams, culture and education were ways of deepening the quality of life and extending democracy by enlarging people's capacities for thinking, criticising, creating and controlling their world. He emphasised the popular, creative and dynamic character of culture in his insistence that

> Culture is ordinary... Every human society has its own shape. Its purposes, its own meanings. Every human society expresses these in institutions and in arts and learning. The making of a society is the finding of common meanings, and directions, and its growth is an active debate and amendment, under the pressures of experience, contact and discovery... the growing society is there, and yet it is also made and remade in every individual mind.[7]

From this perspective, discussions about the relation between the arts and culture start with the recognition of symbolic creativity in everyday, ordinary culture. It is from here that the search for new and expanded audiences for the arts, museums and galleries and libraries ought to begin, not from within institutional perspectives and definitions – from objects and artifacts and from where art thinks is "here" – but with people. The same case is frequently made in relation to adult education – that it should start with learners, rather than with institutional procedures or established knowledge.

Writing specifically about the young, Paul Willis argues that 'creative activity, reflection and expression are in all young people's lives all the time – only they have different names'.[8] He concentrates on young people in his exploration of culture and the arts not only because they are different to other age groups but also to illustrate the point that the lived experience of specific social groups is rich in social and emotional complexity, activity, nuance, meaning and diversity. Lived experience is the context through which people construct themselves in relation to others. Caribbean and Asian traditions are very important to young black people, for example. 'They use their cultural backgrounds as frameworks for living and as repertoires of symbolic resources for interpreting all aspects of their lives.'[9]

This culture is a source of pride to many of them and one of the fundamental means through which they explore what distinguishes them from white youth. In the process they are developing their own identities, re-creating their culture, and affirming their resistance to an omnipresent and exclusionary racism which equates 'being English' with being white. It is complex because 'they are trying to negotiate what it means to be a black person in a white culture at the same time as they are engaged in the same creative activities as their white peers, through which they also explore aspects of their black identities'.[10]

The symbolic creativity involved in making meaning – using language, having feelings, playing roles, producing rituals and performances in relation to others – is a necessary and ordinary human activity. It is important because it ensures the daily production and reproduction of human existence. It reminds us that the nature and character of culture – in relation to race, class, gender, age and religion, for example – are not predetermined, they are learned. But they are also lived, experimented with and changed in the process of pushing up against their established limitations. These are social negotiations which involve conflict, restriction, and power, but also co-operation, resilience and desire. They involve everyone.

To stress the separateness of the arts from everyday life, or to view the world of ordinary people – especially if they are poor, excluded, ill-educated – as a kind of cultural desert in which the humdrum rules, but from which they can be saved by having greater access to arts and culture, misses the extraordinary significance of this necessary and very ordinary activity. It is the wellspring out of which the real force of art originates. But equally, whilst there is an understandable resistance to the elitism and separation of high culture, and a wish to recognise and value everyday meanings in the way in which Williams insisted that culture is ordinary, there are limits to uncritical populism. Lord Reith, the former Director General of the BBC, once commented that 'he who prides himself on giving what he thinks the public wants is often creating a fictitious demand for lower standards, which he will then satisfy'.[11]

Adult educators once worried that working men and women would be too exhausted by manual labour to spend time on education and self-improvement. Now there is an obsession with accessibility, bite-sized chunks and rung-by-rung progression. My experience of teaching working-class people over the last 25 years, however, is that they are critical, challenging and well able to resist being patronised. It is important, therefore, to be sceptical of current trends in popular culture and lifelong learning concerned to rob people of choice, whilst at the same time providing an inferior fare and pretending to be giving them what they want.

An alternative to the elitism of the one and the uncritical populism of the other can benefit from a serious investment in lifelong learning as a majority activity, requiring the democratisation of both art and education in ways that will inevitably involve change. This is a journey which is not about dumbing-down but about expanding cultural, emotional, and intellectual access to knowledge, including the construction of new knowledge. It is a purpose shared by Raymond Williams when he said,

> to take our arts to new audiences is to be quite certain that in many respects these arts will be changed...if we understand cultural growth, we shall know that it is a continual offering for common acceptance; that we should not, therefore, try to determine in advance what should be offered, but clear the channels to let all the offerings be made, taking care to give the difficult full space, the original full time, so that it is a real growth and not just a wider confirmation of old rules.[12]

---

[6] R Williams (1958) 'Culture is Ordinary' in N McKenzie (ed) Conviction, London: Macgibbon and Kee

[7] *ibid*

[8] P Willis (1990) *Common Culture*, Milton Keynes: Open University Press p7

[9] *ibid*

[10] *ibid*

[11] Lord Reith quoted in Nicholas Murray (2000) 'Culture and Accessibility', in *Art for All? Their Policies and Our Culture*, ed Wallinger and Warnock, London: Peer

[12] Williams *op cit*

2
LIFELONG LEARNING

Lifelong learning is now the major policy context in which the British Government seeks to encourage, promote and fund learning for those who are over the age of 16. It is the term increasingly used by those in adult education and the arts and culture sectors to identify the educational focus of their work. According to John Field and Mal Leicester, 'it recurs in the most surprising variety of contexts...and it appears to command respect among those who are otherwise political enemies'.[13]

One reason why lifelong learning can be used with widespread approval is because it glosses over other ways of thinking and speaking about education. Now competing interests and different agendas can shelter together under the same umbrella, providing an illusion of consensus. It allows for turf wars to be suspended and boundaries to be blurred. It carries international authority as the global discourse within which politicians, economic and professional organisations, non-govermental and intergovernmental agencies and educationalists talk about education. As the term gains in popularity, its significance is consolidated.

The attraction of lifelong learning is that it means everything. But because it means everything, it is also in danger of meaning nothing. It is possible to attach it like a kitemark to whatever initiative is seeking approval and especially to initiatives that are seeking government funding. According to Ann Hodgson, lifelong learning has been the contemporary 'response to, or even defence against, a changing frightening and unknown technological, economic and political environment'. It has become a concept 'as slippery and multi-faceted as the environment in which it exists'.[14]

At their meeting in Cologne in 1999, the heads of state of the eight major democracies taking part in the G8 economic summit issued a joint charter of aims and ambitions for lifelong learning. According to the Cologne Charter, because of globalisation, the challenge facing every country is

> how to become a learning society and to ensure its citizens are
> equipped with the knowledge, skills and qualifications they will

need for the next century. Economies and societies are increasingly knowledge-based. Education and skills are indispensable to achieving economic success, civic responsibility and social cohesion.[15]

Of course globalisation is far from being a level playing field – as third world debt, the anti-capitalist protests since Seattle and the ramifications of 11 September 2001 make abundantly clear. Globalisation also creates and accentuates its own contradictions. In the age of the Internet, 80 per cent of the world's population have never made a phone call. In the age of 'enduring freedom' the three richest men in the world have assets that exceed the combined GDP of the 48 poorest nations.[16] But whilst different people and different countries have different experiences of the advantages and disadvantages associated with globalisation, most governments appear to accept its economic implications and social consequences for the provision of education. According to John Field and Mal Leicester,

> Such developments as the rapid diffusion of information and communications technologies, the constant application of science and technology to new fields, and the globalisation of trade in goods and services have made it impossible to rely on existing ways of educating and training the workforce. Hence the need for constant investment in human capital, not simply so that firms and nations can compete but also in order that individuals and regions do not fall behind in the jobs race.[17]

The development of lifelong learning policies across the rich, and to a lesser extent the poor, world are being driven by the urgency and uncertainty of changes taking place in global society, especially economic changes.

In Britain, in the 'Foreword' to the *Learning and Skills Council Prospectus: Learning to Succeed*, the former Secretary of State for Education and Employment, David Blunkett, made it clear that

> in a knowledge-driven economy the continuous updating of skills and the development of lifelong learning will make the difference between success and failure and between competitiveness and decline.[18]

Lifelong learning continues to be regarded by government as a central strategy for promoting work and cultivating the work ethic, as a way of ensuring future prosperity and economic competitiveness and generating the kinds of skills that current and future labour markets require. But lifelong learning is also seen as one way of achieving a more cohesive and inclusive society, in which active citizenship and creativity are valued and social deprivation is defeated. Blunkett again:

> Lifelong learning is essential to sustaining a civilised and cohesive society, in which people can develop as active citizens, where creativity is fostered and communities can be given practical support to overcome generations of disadvantage.[19]

LEARNING TO LABOUR [20]

So far the focus of Government activity in relation to lifelong learning has been concentrated in those areas relating to labour market training, although there continue to be high levels of aspiration and exhortation about wider social and cultural concerns, especially regarding the contribution lifelong learning can make to tackling social exclusion. In practice the preoccupation with economic rather than social outcomes has led to an emphasis on learning to labour, work-related training, participation rates and qualifications, rather than on the wider social and cultural purposes of learning. This concentration has inevitably contributed to a rather narrow, uncritical, economistic and utilitarian understanding of lifelong learning, linked to securing economic competitiveness, at the expense of lifelong learning's other main focus to do with personal and social development and cultural renewal. It is currently a policy agenda that is more concerned with bread than with roses. Its focus on those who are already employed, or employable, tends to concentrate resources on the young at the expense of middle-aged and older learners. Its concern with vocational skills and qualifications diminishes the significance of learning for pleasure, learning for personal fulfilment and learning for social empowerment and change.

In practice, emphasis on increasing prosperity through developing skills for a changing job market also reflects what has become a defining characteristic of globalisation: to raise utopian hopes whilst delivering a dystopian existence.

For example, a single domestic computer can now do the work that required an office of full-time staff 20 years ago. The entire labour market increasingly reflects this development. Two thirds of the jobs created in the UK between 1993 and 1998 were not permanent. In the last 20 years, the notion of a job for life – whether it be in a factory making cars or a university teaching students – has become a thing of the past. The hallmark of the new economic reality is the casualisation of paid labour and the erosion of the idea of a work career.[21]

For those employed in many of these jobs, the emerging workspace is increasingly virtual. The use of domestic personal computers, laptops and mobile phones contributes to the disappearance of old-style, dedicated work space that is separate from the rest of life. Then there are the jobs that Ritzer describes in his McDonaldisation thesis that are characterised by the standardisation of production and consumption, through the application of uniform criteria of efficiency, measurement, predictability and control.[22] Employed in these 'hamburger jobs', it is likely that the majority of workers actually use more skill and ingenuity to manage and make sense of their everyday lives than is required of them in the workplace. But it is a trend that is not only evident in call-centres and franchised fast food outlets. It increasingly underpins the drive for quality control and best value in all of the public services, including education and the arts.[23]

Throughout the post-Second World War period, commentators have documented the ways in which the intrinsic value of work has declined and been replaced with a concentration on the rewards it affords in order to finance leisure interests and activities.[24] The point which emerges most powerfully in all of this literature is the immense attraction offered by the relationship between leisure and consumption, as areas of human fulfilment and enrichment. As the satisfaction to be derived from a job well done is reduced in the work sphere, we can expect the sphere of leisure and culture to take on yet more significance. This is a factor which the utilitarian emphasis on jobs and skills in the post-16 curriculum largely fails to address and why promoting artistic and cultural literacy assumes much greater importance.

LEARNING IS ORDINARY

National policy documents and institutional practices most frequently associate 'learning' with what goes on in formal educational and training provision, in preference to the kind of informal learning that people do without the help of educational institutions, and which they learn from the social dynamics of their lives or from being a part of civil society.[25] This includes the 'learning from experience' that occurs within the privacy of personal and family relationships. But it also includes the intricate web of informal affiliations and associations, as well as more organised clubs, support groups, action groups, interest groups, pressure groups, social movements, community groups and communities of interest, whereby people attach meaning and significance to shared experiences and common understandings with others, and through which their concerns and issues are articulated and acted on. It includes creative and consuming passions, leisure activities and interests, and the potential for developing these in a world in which paid work does not have or has lost many of its intrinsic satisfactions.

The significance of informal learning provides an important corrective to the assumption that learning is little other than a marketable commodity to be dispensed – however flexibly and non-formally – by educational institutions. Informal learning reminds us that learning is ordinary. It is consistent with the social agency of learners who are engaged in the dynamic process of living and making sense of complicated lives, in a wide variety of contexts and different circumstances, in most cases without the services of education. It reminds us that learning occurs throughout life: from books; from television and the Internet; from visiting theatres and galleries and museums; from writing or painting or collecting objects as a private passion.

Of course, formal and non-formal education ought to make extraordinary sense of some of this ordinary activity and experience. It should help to examine critically what is already known. It should add new insight and different knowledge. It should help people to use their creativity and their agency more effectively. It should support the development of a more informed, intelligent, thoughtful and just society. But in an economic and institutional climate preoccupied with work skills and vocational qualifications, imaginative, creative and democratic ways of expanding the possibilities of social and cultural education have to be argued for and defended energetically. As Paolo Freire frequently insisted, education ought to assist people in the practice of freedom rather than conform them to the logic of the present system.

Recognising the important relationship between informal and formal learning should remind us to put learners at the heart of learning, as the subjects of learning rather than the objects of policy interventions of one kind or another. They should be regarded as experienced, creative and knowledgeable social actors, rather than empty vessels. The idea of a 'citizen' is much more appropriate in this respect than the now-familiar 'audience' or 'consumer'. Recognising the significance of informal learning should also encourage us to think more critically about the nature and permeability of the boundaries between institutions and the citizens they serve, and about what learning and participation actually means, in the context of cultural renewal.

NOT FIXING THE PLUMBING

In a recent interview, Claire Rayner explained why, after many years of being an agony aunt, receiving as many as 1,000 letters a week, she had given it all up to become a campaigner. It was, she said, because in her experience, most people's problems stemmed from being poor or unemployed, living in a lousy environment, or being on the receiving end of abuse and violence. Continuing to respond to these as 'individual problems' was rather like 'mopping up the water on the kitchen floor without fixing the plumbing'.[26]

Too much of the current debate about increasing participation in lifelong learning and arts and culture also smacks of 'not fixing the plumbing'. The process is preoccupied – allegedly – with responding to the needs of individuals. Paying close attention to the individuality and diversity of potential learners, in an audit culture greedy to bag numerical targets is – if it is true – enormously important. Otherwise people become, quite simply, new audiences or bums on seats. But valuing diversity and individuality is rather different from encouraging individualism with all its privatising, pathologising and self-centred overtones and which has the effect of turning public issues – such as poverty, racism, inequality – back into private troubles. The Cologne Charter, for example, is very clear that whilst governments should increase their investments in education and training – especially in partnership with business and the private sector – it is 'the responsibility of individuals' to 'develop their own abilities and career' on the basis of 'self-generated learning' and by means of 'modern and effective ICT networks' and 'distance learning'.[27]

The Charter addresses itself briefly to the needs of the disadvantaged, to civic responsibility and social cohesion in ways that assume consensus but without any recognition of the considerable ideological and actual disagreement about the meanings of these terms and the values underpinning their realisation. The socially-excluded are labelled collectively but approached individually. The attention is directed to first-rung, self-help and individual responsibilities, all of which underestimate the impact of structural constraints and overlook the huge disparity in resources available to different social groups – both of which affect their capacities to change their circumstances on an individual basis.

New Labour is committed to reducing social exclusion and clearly understands that social and structural forces ensure that poverty is not exactly people's fault,[28] But the response is usually in terms of individual responsibilities. In asking 'how we empower people to cope with change' and 'renew our civic society' Tony Blair, in a pre-election speech, 'insisted' that it was 'the duty' of individuals 'to make the most of the chances they get' and declared 'individual responsibility' to be 'the key to social order'.[29]

There are two dangers in this tendency, which seems to regard society as an aggregation of individuals, who are invariably referred to separately as solitary rather than social agents. Not only does it relegate discussions about 'common struggles' and 'common interests' to the dustbin of history, but it also translates aspirations for cultural renewal and critical engagement with political processes into issues of self-fulfilment, confidence-building, consumer choice, employability and volunteering.[30] It also appears to 'require' participation in ways that are determined to adjust the socially excluded to the norms and values of white middle-class society – through education, re-training, volunteering, voting – in ways that rely on more than a little coercion and which tolerate few excuses from those who do not want to participate in this way. The danger here is that the blame

for social exclusion and poverty is placed on apathetic or wilful non-par-
ticipating individuals rather than on wider structural and societal trends
and influences.

Thus, whilst lifelong learning has become a convenient shorthand, used by
policy-makers, providers and practitioners to describe the modernising of
education and training systems for the future, and has enjoyed increasing
prominence in related arts and culture policy discussions, it remains
controversial. It is not a 'big idea' that has so far provoked much enthusiasm
among those who are the potential recipients of its intended benefits,
especially those who know from their own experience that education has
failed to make a qualitative difference to their lives in the past. They will
need a lot of persuading that lifelong learning will be any different.

The big challenge facing those of us who are enthusiastic about the liber-
ating potential of education, arts and culture, and who are committed to
their redistribution as valuable and useful resources for qualitatively better lives and progressive social change is to remind all those involved that
people need bread and roses to enhance the quality of their lives, in ways
that are relevant to their urgent problems and real concerns and which lift
their spirits in difficult and troubled times.

---

[13] J Field and M Leicester eds (2000) *Lifelong Learning: Education Across the
Lifespan*, London: Routledge Falmer

[14] A Hodgson (2000) *Policies, Politics and the Future of Lifelong Learning*, London:
Kogan Page

[15] G8 (1999) *Cologne Charter: Aims and Ambitions for Lifelong Learning*, G8 Summit:
Cologne

[16] D Muddiman *et al* (2000) *Open to All? The Public Library and Social Exclusion*,
London: Resource

[17] J Field and M Leicester (2000) Introduction, *Lifelong Learning: Education Across
the Lifespan*, London: Routledge Falmer

[18] DfEE (1999) *The Learning and Skills Council Prospectus: Learning to Succeed*,
London: DfEE

[19] *ibid*

[20] I Martin (2001) 'Lifelong learning – For Earning, Yawning or Yearning?' in *Adults
Learning*, Vol 13, Number 2, October, Leicester: NIACE

[21] V Bayliss (1998) *Redefining Work*, London: Royal Society for the Encouragement
of the Arts

[22] G Ritzer (1992) *The McDonaldisation of Society*, Thousand Oaks: Pine Forge

[23] G Ritzer (1998) 'McUniversity and the Postmodern Consumer Society', *in The McDonaldisation Thesis: Explorations and Extensions*, chapter 11, London: Sage Publications

[24] C Rojek (2000) *Leisure and Culture*, Basingstoke: Nalgrave

[25] For the purposes of this discussion I am using the different definitions of learning noted by Benseman, Findsen and Scott (1996) *The Fourth Sector: Adult and Community Education in New Zealand*, Palmerston North: Dunmore Press p58. 'Formal learning refers to any purposefully organised learning process which is substantially controlled by the institution in or through which it is delivered. Non-formal learning refers to any purposefully organised learning process which is intended to serve an identifiable group with specific learning objectives and which is substantially controlled by the participants and/or local community. Informal learning refers to learning processes which are ongoing, pervasive and incidental'.

[26] Claire Rayner interviewed by Anthony Claire, *In the Psychiatrist's Chair*, BBC Radio 4, 19 October, 2001.

[27] *Cologne Charter: Aims and Ambitions for Lifelong Learning* (1999) G8 Summit, Cologne

[28] See, for example, *Bringing Britain Back Together; a National Strategy for Neighbourhood Renewal*, SEU 1998

[29] Tony Blair 8 February 2001

[30] See, for example, David Blunkett, 'From strength to strength: rebuilding the community through voluntary action', speech to the Annual Conference of the National Council for Voluntary Organisations, 7 February 2001

3
ARTS, CULTURE AND EDUCATION

Most arts and cultural organisations now recognise that, whether they like it or not, they are involved in education. What people can learn from them is no longer simply implicit in the process of storing, staging, producing and presenting various kinds of collections, exhibits and performances. It has become an activity in its own right, and part of wider attempts to attract and retain new audiences, participants and funders. Education in the context of arts and culture can mean many things. It can refer to formal work with the education sector, or with young people, or to events aimed at the general public and designed to provide context and interpretation. At times it is used interchangeably with the term "outreach" to cover activities aimed at specific groups in the local community who represent a new or different audience and with the notion of access to provide experiences relating to the arts aimed at those who are not usually participants. It is often mentioned in the same breath as audience development or marketing with dreadful references to "the pulling power" of different approaches.

In the world of libraries, archives and museums, it is frequently assumed that, through their collections, these are institutions that *support* the learning which takes place elsewhere – in schools and colleges or adult education classes, for example. But this is to underestimate the educative power of cultural providers in their own right. Visitors and learners are just as likely to find their way to archives, library and museum services under their own steam, to feed their own informal interests in local or family history, reading or historical collections, whether or not they are engaged in educational activities elsewhere. The more that user-centred information and imaginitive activities relating to collections are in place, the more tangible the educational contributions of these services appear to be. But deliberate educational interventions by cultural service providers reflect scarcely the tip of the iceberg compared to the informal learning, curiosity and interest which visitors to libraries and museums ordinarily exhibit for their own purposes. In addition, because visiting libraries, archives and museums involves voluntary activity, associated with information-gathering, consuming passions, entertainment and pleasure, they are not associated in the public consciousness with education with a capital E. For this reason, their potential contribution to the expansion of informal and non-formal learning opportunities is enormous.

The intention of arts and cultural education can be to provide existing and potential audiences with the tools to understand, appreciate and enjoy the arts; it can provide direct experience of the arts as a means of personal or social development; or it can use education as a way of achieving specific organisational aims, such as attracting new audiences or supporting wider policy objectives. In tune with current government preoccupations, it is argued that enormous social benefits are to be derived from arts and cultural education, in terms of personal development, social cohesion and community empowerment, which can contribute to every area of social policy.[31] Looked at from a more independent and radical perspective, the role of the artist as social and political critic is dignified by history and precedent in ways that have an important educational dimension and a consequent contribution to make to cultural action, cultural democracy and active citizenship. Community arts and street theatre, for example, have a lot to offer the development of what philosopher Martha Nussbaum[32] calls 'the narrative imagination' as well as bringing pleasure and participation on their own terms to people in their own communities.

Coming together with others in cultural and educational activities, to define common, unfulfilled desires and needs, and to identify the forces that frustrate them, can be a powerful tonic for the imagination. This sense of common purpose and intention to make a difference is the stuff of social transformation – both in learning and in art. In those words and images and symbols, whereby people recognise themselves and name their condition in the company of others – in ways that celebrate difference, generate understanding and encourage activity – lie the possibility, not simply of resistance to being ill-served, but of the energy to create something better.

Nussbaum identifies three qualities as necessary for creative citizenship in a complex world: an ability to examine oneself and one's traditions critically; an ability to see beyond immediate group loyalties and to extend to strangers the moral concern we 'naturally' extend to friends and kin; and the development of what she calls 'the narrative imagination' – the ability to see unobvious connections between sequences of human actions, and to recognise their likely consequences, intended and unintended. Nussbaum believes that these three qualities help to sustain the political health of a democratic society and can be encouraged by purposeful and committed kinds of creative learning.

The close analysis of situations drawn from the lived experience of ourselves and others through the creative arts requires us to reflect critically on their meaning and implications. It liberates our imaginations, she says, to explore experiences other than our own, in ways that can expand our moral comprehension. Once the narrative imagination is at work, it becomes possible to contemplate unobvious connections and a whole range of possible outcomes. Such analyses help us to know ourselves more exactly and more critically and to stand in another's shoes with greater insight and understanding.[33]

Once citizens and learners come to know themselves and others, as social actors and as members of communities, in ways that resist externally-defined and often internalised stereotyping, they are at the beginning of a critique of culture and society. If deep-seated and often powerful personal alienation or prejudice can be translated into critical thinking, the door becomes wide open to imagination and transformation.

Whatever the purpose of arts and cultural education, and however formally or informally conceived, it does not, as yet, provide an educational service to the whole community. Arts organisations, museums and libraries carry a specific cultural cache that is more accessible to some sections of society than others. For example, only 30 per cent of the population are library users, two out of three of whom are middle-class.[34] Less than 5 per cent of the population makes half the total museum and gallery visits made each year.[35] The class and ethnic profile of those who regularly participate in arts and cultural activities of various kinds is not vastly different to the class composition and ethnic background of those who take part in adult learning.[36] Not surprisingly, those who are the poorest, least-educated, not economically active, most marginalised, and those whose cultural identities are hardest to negotiate in a predominantly white and middle-class ambience, are least likely to believe that such activities have anything to do with them. Arguments for widening participation and combating social exclusion, already implicit in the ambitious vision of the learning society, are just as critical when it comes to providing arts and cultural services that are genuinely open to all.

Arguments about widening participation and expanding education remain contentious, however. In most cases, the areas of work designated as education do not constitute what is commonly understood as the core artistic exhibit or programme of an arts or cultural organisation. When educational approaches are added on to services, they are often the consequence of pragmatism and political expediency. They are not usually about developing the potential and commitment of the institution on behalf of all citizens. They are more often about making small adjustments to avoid more fundamental changes. In practice, educational approaches take various forms and are a response to a mixture of circumstances including idealism, opportunism, pressure from funders and pressure from government. Most significantly, since the change of government in 1997, the demand has increased that publicly-funded arts organisations, libraries, archives, museums and galleries, should contribute to the creation of a more socially inclusive society, partly through lifelong learning and partly through combating social exclusion.

Whilst ministerial speeches inevitably reduce the underlying philosophy of such policy directives and proposed developments to a series of soundbites, to be picked up by the media, in ways that inevitably strike an instrumental chord, a recent speech by the Arts Minister, Tessa Blackstone, makes it pretty clear which way the wind is blowing. Outlining her vision for the future of the arts in a speech at the Cheltenham Festival of Literature in 2001, she said,

> I believe that the arts are worthwhile and worth supporting in their own sake. But they also have the power to develop human potential. They can therefore play a part in improving the position of disadvantaged groups and areas by contributing to better educational performance; better employability and employment; more law-abiding activity; and better health.[37]

She went on to list four key objectives for the arts:

- excellence: the need to sustain and encourage the very best in the arts and culture

- access: making quality cultural activity available to as many people as possible

- education: making sure artistic creativity forms a central part of individuals' learning experience

- ensuring the creative economy becomes an increasingly vital part of our national economy.

Beyond these simple objectives lies the New Labour vision of a learning society fit for the 21st century, in which lifelong learning, social cohesion and responsible citizenship hold the key to economic prosperity and social inclusion. It is not simply that organisations and institutions which receive public subsidy should become increasingly accessible to more and different citizens, as a matter of principle and social equity, but also the belief that they have a distinctive role to play in reaching the parts that more formal educational provision and social policy initiatives struggle to reach.

A number of claims are made about the value of arts and cultural activities in relation to community development. These include:

- cultural activity is an infinitely diverse route to personal development in people of all ages, leading to enhanced skills, confidence and creativity

- cultural action helps to build community capacity, empowers local groups and stimulates active, engaged citizenship

- culture brings people together in celebration, exploration and community and is a key factor in family life and settlement

- because identity is built from the stories we tell to ourselves and about ourselves: culture is essential to creating a confident, cohesive and questioning identity

- culture is a major source of wealth, estimated by DCMS as representing around £60 billion of economic activity annually. The creative industries have recorded an annual growth rate above 7 per cent over the past decade and are expected to play a key role in future economic success

In much the same way, libraries, archives, museums and galleries have become the focus of a series of reports and recommendations emanating from the DCMS which encourage them to re-invent themselves as agents for social change, and to become more proactive in developing the public service side of their work.[38] All are being encouraged to work in partnership with each other.[39] Local authorities are asked to consider how such services can contribute to tackling social exclusion and how best to foster cooperative activities between the libraries, museums, galleries and archives in their areas. Outreach activities are increasingly recommended, involving advocacy and consultation with local people and excluded groups.

In April 2000, the government agency Resource was launched to work with museums and galleries, archives and libraries in the UK to encourage these developments, to promote institutional collaboration and to focus specifically on issues concerning education, inclusion, access and diversity.

[31] F Matarasso (1997) *Use or Ornament? The Social Impact of Participation in the Arts*, London: Comedia

[32] M Nussbaum (1997) *Cultivating Humanity: A Classical Defense of Reform in Liberal Education*. Cambridge, Massachussetts: Harvard University Press

[33] *ibid*

[34] D Muddiman *et al* (2000) *Open to All? The Public Library and Social Exclusion*, London: Resource

[35] *Renaissance in the Regions; A New Vision for England's Museums* (2001) DCMS

[36] See, for example, N Sargant (2000) *The Learning Divide Revisited; a Report on the Findings of a UK Wide Survey on Adult Participation in Education and Learning*, Leicester: NIACE

[37] T Blackstone, 19 October 2001

[38] See, for example, DCMS (2001) *Libraries, Museums, Galleries and Archives For All*

[39] See, for example, the Government's response to *Empowering the Learning Community*, DCMS March 2001

CHRIS FROM
BEDFORD FO
PURSUING HI
INTEREST IN
WARRIORS O
PART OF THE
TONGUES OF E
PROJECT, INV
HOMELESS Y
PEOPLE.

BEDFORD MUSEU
CECIL HIGGINS A

Culture, Policy
and
Social Change

4
POVERTY AND SOCIAL EXCLUSION

Imagine living on half an average income. It would obviously involve a fairly basic standard of living. But almost 14 million people in Britain live in households in which income is below this level. This is at least 20 per cent of the population (compared to 8 per cent in 1979) and includes over 4 million children. In the last 20 years poverty in Britain has increased – not only in terms of the numbers of people involved, but also in its severity. The real incomes of the poorest 10 per cent of the population actually declined by 17 per cent between 1979 and 1995 and have continued to do so.[40]

An early investigation into poverty and social exclusion in the new millenium by researchers for the Joseph Rowntree Foundation and the Office of National Statistics found that

- 9.5 million people cannot afford to keep their homes adequately heated

- 8 million people cannot afford one or more essential household goods such as a fridge, a telephone or carpets

- around 4 million people are not fed properly by today's standards

- some 6.5 million adults go without essential clothing such as a warm waterproof coat because of lack of money

- about 10 million adults cannot afford regular savings

- almost 7.5 million are too poor to engage in social activities [41]

The research confirms that more than one in three children is experiencing multiple deprivation and poverty at a time when the Government is aiming to eliminate child poverty within a generation. It demonstrates that poverty rates are highest in homes where no adult has any work at all or works only part-time; in lone-parent households; in large families; in families where someone is chronically sick or disabled and in families of non-white ethnic origin. Using the kinds of indicators which derive from limited income and lack of material resources, the research team estimates that 26 per cent of the population are living in poverty – including 71 per cent of unemployed people, 61 per cent of long-term sick and disabled people and 62 per cent of lone parents.

Subsequent studies have confirmed these statistics and added others. London has the highest proportion of poor people of any region in England but also has the highest proportion of rich people. The overall number of people who would like paid work is much higher than those officially unemployed (4.5 million compared to 1.5 million). Whereas the numbers of officially unemployed have halved since 1993, the number who are 'economically inactive but would like work' has remained unchanged. Ten million adults who are not in paid work or full-time education do not participate in any social, political, cultural or community organisations. One in six of the poorest households still do not have any type of bank/building society account, compared with one in 20 households on average incomes. Over one million pensioners are completely dependent on the state retirement pension and state benefits. The proportion of elderly households helped to live at home by social services has been falling since 1994. The number of households in temporary accommodation continues to rise and is now higher than at any other time over the last decade.[42]

According to Professor Johnathan Bradshaw, the director of the first of these studies,

> high rates of social deprivation have the effects of worsening health, education, and job skills, as well as relationships within families, between ethnic groups, and across society as a whole. If Britain is become an inclusive society in which everybody has a stake and is able to participate then the most important task facing government is the ending of poverty and social exclusion.[43]

Whilst the Government recognises the seriousness of this situation and has introduced a wide range of initiatives to tackle poverty and social exclusion, including the national strategy for neighbourhood renewal, 'it is not yet clear whether the initiatives are collectively sufficient to address the scale and depth of the problems over time' or 'how successful they are in helping the disadvantaged to catch up – or at least keep up – with the rest of society'.[44]

Meanwhile policy-makers and opinion-leaders have lost no time in rearranging themselves around ideas of opportunity and the value of diversity, by bringing some working class/black/women/gay individuals closer to the centres of power, whilst limiting at an alarming rate the space for active democratic engagement by the majority. A smorgasbord of lifestyles, with token recognition paid to difference and identity, may give the appearance of an equal society, but assimilation and variety do not shift the overall balance of power unless they are attached to the activity of redistribution.

Social exclusion is now routinely used as a social category and contributes to a discourse that both describes and covers a multitude of sins. It is defined by the Social Exclusion Unit as 'a shorthand label for what can happen when individuals or areas suffer from a combination of linked problems such as unemployment, poor skills, low incomes, poor housing, high crime environments, bad health and family breakdown'. But this is a definition which concentrates on 'problems' that are 'suffered from' rather like misfortunes or the symptoms of an illness. It ignores causation. As such it acts as a convenient euphemism for a number of conditions that are both socially and politically less palatable such as structural inequality, absolute poverty and the divisions created by social class. All of them are conditions which are exacerbated by other, equally unfashionable, concerns such as oppression, discrimination, exploitation and racism.

In these circumstances, the concept of social exclusion allows us to talk about and target individuals and groups of individuals such as the long-term unemployed, pregnant teenagers, disaffected youth, minority ethnic communities, people with disabilities, one-parent families, refugees, asylum-seekers, homeless people, the dependent elderly, addicts, people with mental health problems and prisoners, in terms of the stereotypes they inhabit and the problems they pose. It prevents us from worrying too much about what they have in common with each other, other than the fact that they seem to be concentrated in the country's poorest regions, run-down neighbourhoods and worst estates. To paraphrase a better-known aphorism – there is now no such thing as social class or racial inequality, only individuals and groups of individuals who are socially excluded.

I am not arguing, of course, that in terms of adult learning, arts and culture, we should not work to change to all of this, but that we should begin with some of the assumptions that influence the ways in which social exclusion is commonly perceived. It is always much easier to blame the victims rather than change the system, after all. The focus on the deficiencies of individuals and minority groups, however well intentioned, distracts attention away from the structural, social, political and economic circumstances, and trends, which give rise to social inequalities and which are largely outside the control of those who live in poor communities. It also avoids the close scrutiny of institutional cultures in both education and the arts, which may not be intentionally, but are frequently inherently, exclusive.

In these circumstances, we probably need rather less in the way of targeting the socially excluded via short-term initiatives that effectively serve institutional funding interests, and rather more in the way of sustained alliances between education and cultural workers and local people in pursuit of heightened social and political awareness, critical understanding and social change.

---

[40] Social Exclusion Unit (1999) *Bringing Britain Back Together; a National Strategy for Neighbourhood Renewal*, London: HMSO; United Nations Children's Fund (2000) *Poverty Begins with Children*, New York: UNICEF

[41] Joseph Rowntree Foundation (2000) *Poverty and Social Exclusion in Britain*, York: York Publishing Services

[42] M Rahman, G Palmer and P Kenway (2001) *Monitoring Poverty and Social Exclusion*, Joseph Rowntree Foundation

[43] Joseph Rowntree Foundation, *op cit*

[44] Rahman *et al*, *op cit*

5

REPORTS AND RECOMMENDATIONS

The activity of the Social Exclusion Unit (SEU), since its creation by Tony Blair in 1997, is an important place to start looking for clues to New Labour's policy approach to social exclusion. One of the SEU's first responsibilities in 1997 was to develop integrated and sustainable approaches to the problems of the worst housing estates, including crime, drugs, unemployment, community breakdown and bad housing. In response to this challenge, a report entitled *Bringing Britain Back Together: a National Strategy for Neighbourhood Renewal* was published in 1998, analysing the major problems facing deprived neighbourhoods. In order to develop a national strategy for neighbourhood renewal at local, regional and national levels, the SEU then established 18 Policy Action Teams (PATs) to carry out fieldwork and come up with some recommendations.

POLICY ACTION TEAM 10

Policy Action Team 10 (PAT 10) was concerned with 'using the arts, sports and leisure to engage people in poor neighbourhoods, particularly those who may feel most excluded' and with 'maximising the impact of government spending and policies' in such areas. Its main findings in relation to the arts include the recognition that:

- participation, and the provision of services to support participation, in the arts can help address neighbourhood renewal by improving communities' 'performance' on the four key indicators of more jobs, less crime, better health and improved educational attainment.

- there are various distinctive contributions which the arts have to offer to tackling the causes of social exclusion. These can be summarised under the headings of: growing industries; engaging and strengthening local communities; and an emphasis on people, not buildings or places.

- however, these significant benefits are frequently overlooked both by some providers of arts facilities and programmes, and by those involved in area regeneration programmes, and barriers remain.

In addition:

- projects are often focused on the requirements of particular funding organisations or programmes rather than on the needs of those on the receiving end.

- they are often funded on a short-term basis, whereas a longer period will often be needed for sustainable benefits to accrue.

- arts bodies tend to regard community development work as being both an 'add-on' to their 'real' work and as a lesser form of activity.

- other bodies involved in regeneration tend to regard the arts as peripheral; regeneration projects tend to focus on changing the physical environment, and to pay insufficient attention to building individual and collective 'self-help' capacity-building within the community.

- there is a lack of available evaluated information about the regenerative aspects of arts-based community development projects and lack of information in accessible formats about facilities/funds available to community groups and people/groups at risk of social exclusion.

In coming to these conclusions, PAT 10 identified a number of working principles which, it was thought, should inform future developments. These include:

valuing diversity: people have a basic right to explore their own culture and identity in terms and forms which they choose and determine.

embedding local control: models which offer control to those who are involved, albeit in partnership with funding agencies, local authorities and other stakeholders, are likely to have a much deeper impact on those involved and the wider community

supporting local commitment: the most effective initiatives are those where local enthusiasm/participation and voluntary commitment/engagement can be matched appropriately by the support of local authorities and partners in the voluntary, educational, cultural or business sectors

promoting equitable partnerships: fair partnerships should ensure an equitable distribution of risks and benefits among all those involved

defining common objectives in relation to actual needs: all those involved should have shared – or, at least, not incompatible – objectives, relating directly to local needs

working flexibly with change: one of the great weaknesses of arts funding systems is inertia – it is essential to retain a degree of flexibility so that new responses can be offered to new situations

securing sustainability: short-termism and partial funding is not adequate – there is a need to build in systems of support for services rather than projects

pursuing quality across the spectrum: community development work should not be conceived in terms which stigmatise or condescend to those in the neighbourhoods concerned.

connecting with the mainstream: arts community development initiatives should be connected to the wider social inclusion and community development agenda and to mainstream arts development.

A significant report published in 1997 by the independent research body Comedia has also been influential in supporting arguments for the wider social benefits of arts activities. *Use or Ornament? The Social Impact of Participation in the Arts*[45] showed that participation in the arts contributes to community development and active citizenship in a number of ways. For example:

- it is an effective route for personal growth, leading to enhanced confidence, skill building and educational developments which can improve people's social contacts and employability

- it can contribute to social cohesion by developing networks and understanding, and building local capacity for organisation and self-determination

- it brings benefits in other areas such as environmental renewal and health promotion, and injects an element of creativity into organisational planning

- it produces social change which can be seen, evaluated and broadly planned

- it represents a flexible, responsive and cost-effective element of community development strategy

- it strengthens Britain's cultural life and informs a vital factor of success rather than a soft option in social policy.

The study concluded that a marginal adjustment of priorities in cultural and social policy could deliver real socio-economic benefits to people and communities and recommended a framework for developing the role of participatory arts initiatives in public policy.

Neither the PAT 10 nor the Comedia report had much to say about the contribution of museums and galleries to the social exclusion agenda and they make no reference at all to archives or libraries. However, DCMS and Resource have been swift to relate the findings and working principles of PAT 10 to others in the culture sector. For example:

Libraries for All [46] was the first DCMS policy guidance on the issue to any of the services covered in its remit. It stated that social inclusion should be mainstreamed as a policy priority for all public library services and recommended a strategy based on a six-point plan to address social exclusion. Later the policy guidance was supplemented by Libraries, Museums, Galleries and Archives for All [47] in which all were invited to see themselves as 'agents for social change'.

Using Museums, Archives and Libraries to Develop a Learning Community.[48] This Resource Action Plan includes policy relating to inclusion, access and diversity. The link it makes between learning and inclusion is important as learning is widely acknowledged as being the key to unlocking the potential of excluded people and the communities in which they live.

REPORTING ON LIBRARIES

1 / *Open to All? The Public Library and Social Exclusion*[49], published by Resource, was the result of a major research project into Public Libraries and Social Inclusion carried out by Leeds Metropolitan University, Merton Libraries, Sheffield Libraries and John Vincent. The research report identified a conservative profession, with managers ill-informed about the issues involved and reluctant to change. They found ideas about access to be built largely on mainstream middle-class, white and English values which have led to

- considerable under-use of the library service by working-class people and other excluded groups

- lack of knowledge within the service about the needs and views of non-users

- the institution of organisational, cultural and environmental barriers which effectively exclude many groups

- a reluctance to adopt resourcing models that consistently prioritise excluded communities and social groups

- a preoccupation with libraries as a passive service which adopts a take-it-or-leave-it approach to access rather than a proactive, interventionist and educative approach.

The report revealed that only 16 per cent of local authorities in 2000 had developed an effective service-wide policy addressing social exclusion and that 24 per cent were doing almost nothing to address the issues involved. In addition, some of the most marginal and stigmatised groups – including refugees, homeless people and travellers – were not considered to be priority participants so far as most library authorities are concerned. The core conclusion of the study was that whilst public libraries have the potential to play a key role in tackling social exclusion, in order to make a real difference they need to undergo rapid transformation and change.

The Social Exclusion Action Planning Network was subsequently set up by the research team to assist public libraries and other organisations to tackle social exclusion through interaction with their local communities. This is being achieved by:

- putting the research findings of *Open to All?* and related policy initiatives into practice

- providing information on current social exclusion initiatives and exploring how these may be applied to public libraries and related local services

- drawing on current practice, exploring relevant developments and good practice, recording and sharing these within the Network and more widely

- helping to create opportunities for developing joint approaches to tackling social exclusion.

The Network provides training courses and seminars, consultancies, and a monthly newsletter and now has over 60 member organisations.

2/ *Empowering the Learning Community*[50], a report produced by the Library Information Commission (now subsumed within Resource), has raised rather different concerns about inefficiencies in the co-ordination of library services. The report was convinced that greater collaboration between library services would 'bring maximum benefit to otherwise easily excluded groups'. In order to achieve this ambition:

- public and educational libraries in communities or defined geographic areas should establish co-operative arrangements to improve services to their users

- cross-sectoral funding arrangements should be established. Funding for libraries in all sectors should include an element which is measured against progress towards cross-sectoral community partnerships

- public and educational libraries in any community or region should draw up 'access maps' to enable users and learners to reach resources or assistance in other libraries on a managed basis

- training programmes for librarians, resource managers and teachers should be co-ordinated and should include ways of developing mutual support. Objective and quantifiable performance measures should be set for all these collaborative strategies

3 / *The Policy Advisory Group's First Report on Social Exclusion*[51], produced for the Library Association (now subsumed within CILIP), paid tribute to the excellent work in relation to social inclusion already being done both within and outside the library and information sector, and acknowledged many examples of good practice. However, the library professionals responsible for the report also drew attention to widespread complacency, caution, introspection and widely differing degrees of commitment and achievement in combating social exclusion across the sector.

The report called for a fundamental commitment to social justice and a practical approach to identifying the causes and facts of exclusion in ways that take account of inequalities in information, learning opportunities, health, economic activity and quality of life. The report also insisted that the involvement of people who experience exclusion should be central to any strategy to address their exclusion.

As well as identifying and working with those who are excluded, the report argued for more critical understanding within the library service about the institutional barriers that prevent use of library services. This is not simply about opening hours or appropriate physical access, but also about culture, the nature of services and the manner in which they are delivered. The barriers also include, for instance, racism, xenophobia and sexism, as well as lack of access to power and resources.

If the library and information service is to reach its potential in tackling social exclusion then there needs to be:

- a cultural transformation in institutions providing library and information services so that social inclusion becomes integral to the planning and delivery of their services

- a policy development infrastructure to support the cultural transformation required

- mainstreaming of social inclusion priorities, not only at the institutional level but also into national thinking to ensure that all programmes are sustainable and inclusive of the whole nation.

Services need to consider, and change as necessary, their existing organisational shape and character to become relevant and useful to a wider range of users and potential users by, for instance,

- working in partnerships and multi-disciplinary teams, both strategic and delivery, to combine resources, share skills, add value and combine professional practices as necessary to achieve 'what works' – such partnerships will include not only other library sectors, museums and archives but a much wider cross-section of agencies including, for instance, health, social services, youth, arts, and community organisations

- involving the user community as much as possible (and not just those with whom the service and staff are in a comfortable relationship) in the planning of operational services

- promoting the best involvement of all staff as appropriate; and resources in the community through the use of volunteers to support the growth of local social capital, community empowerment and the democratisation of local services through local involvement.

The *Public Libraries, Ethnic Diversity and Citizenship*[52] research carried out by Patrick Roach and Marlene Morrison from the University of Warwick remains one of the few national studies into public library engagement with minority ethnic groups. Although fairly specific in its remit, the research study together with its recommendations, and the 'baseline for good practice' developed as a later project, provide a model for approaching the needs of all excluded groups. The research results demonstrate that public libraries are not meeting the needs of most minority ethnic communities and, amongst the recommendations, is a call to re-establish the principle and practice of community librarianship.

The relevance and importance of Roach and Morrison's research has been highlighted more recently by the Stephen Lawrence Inquiry which illustrated the pernicious nature of institutional racism, and led to a reform in English law extending the provisions of the Race Relations Act (to the police force, for instance) and toughening its provisions in relation to all public sector services. The recommendations of the Lawrence Inquiry have also been influential to others in the public sector – further education colleges for instance – in establishing the Report's relevance to a wide range of public institutions.

REPORTING ON MUSEUMS AND GALLERIES

1 / *Museums and Social Inclusion: the GLLAM Report*[53] was published by the Research Centre for Museums and Galleries at Leicester University and provides valuable insight into some of the interesting work being done within the Group for Large Local Authority Museums (GLLAM) to promote social inclusion. Whilst the political contextualising and critical analysis of these developments leaves a lot to be desired in the research commentary, some attempts are made to evaluate them in relation to their impact on individuals and communities. The report concludes that museums can not only have an impact on the four usually cited indicators linked to exclusion – health, crime, unemployment and education – but can also play a wider and even unique role in tackling disadvantage, inequality and discrimination.

However, the researchers found that 'those museums where all staff have a clear idea and a holistic vision about the scope and nature of their work towards social inclusion are rare...lack of support, lack of funding, and lack of clear policies and direction combine with the fuzziness and ambiguity of the concept of social inclusion itself, leading to a situation where the good work being done is frequently invisible'.[54] Whilst some changes are beginning to make a difference, the researchers warn that 'reflecting current diversity is never going to be a matter of labels and décor. Changes in collecting policies, curatorial practices, displays, facilities, staff attitudes, training activities, governing body attitudes, programmes and events, require new skills, courage and risk-taking'.[55]

2 / In October 2001, *Renaissance in the Regions: A New Vision for England's Museums* was published by the Regional Task Force, set up by Chris Smith in December 2000 to look at museums and galleries in the English regions. It recommended that the Government should invest up to £267.2 million over the next five years to revitalise regional museums and galleries.

There are currently 1,860 registered museums and galleries in England, ranging from the biggest national institutions to local and community museums and one-room galleries. They remain popular visitor attractions with as many as 77 million visits made to them each year, including tourists and schoolchildren. However, the latest attendance figures for the regions show a downward trend compared to the growth in visitors to London museums and galleries over the same period. Whilst a third of all adults have visited a museum or gallery in the past year, only 20 to 30 per cent of these are regular visitors. Those who visit are more likely to be middle-class and better educated than the population as a whole: as few as 5 per cent of the population makes almost half of all visits. Overseas visitors account for a further 23 per cent of all visits.

The report describes museum and gallery services in the regions – with some notable exceptions – as being fragmented, under financial pressure, and experiencing low morale, staff shortages, a decline in scholarship and weak leadership. These are problems which are well-known and reflect the consequences of under-resourcing and at least a generation of neglect by politicians and policy-makers. The report comments that whilst

> museums and galleries have an important role to play in education, learning, access, social inclusion, the regions and the modernisation of public services…museums and galleries have to be revitalised to become focal points for excellence…in cooperation with other local and community museums and forging creative and dynamic relationships with university and national museums. Their collections and spaces must be opened up for all to use in a creative way for learning, inspiration and enjoyment.

In these circumstances, the report calls for a strategic approach to revitalising the role of museums and galleries in the regions as a contribution to Government regional and regeneration agendas and to maximising their potential for education and social inclusion. Five major aims, in recognition of Government economic and lifelong learning priorities, are identified:

- to champion learning and education and to support both informal and formal learning at all levels

- to promote access and inclusion that is representative of local populations, including ICT resources for virtual visits and outreach strategies to engage local people in making their own history

- to contribute to economic regeneration in the regions by helping to establish each region's identity and sense of place and by providing opportunities for young people to develop appropriate skills

- to encourage inspiration and creativity in ways that reveal the connections between the past, the present and the future and which encourage and support the development of skills relevant to the creative economy

- to ensure excellence and quality in delivery of core services by developing centres of excellence to develop and spread good practice.

The report recommends a model to secure this agenda which fits astutely with Government inclinations when it comes to delivering social change. The proposal is to create a centre of excellence or hub in each of the nine English regions comprised of one leading museum or gallery and up to three satellites. Each hub should be given additional funding from Government over a five-year period, managed by Resource, to cover additional staffing, to create new access, outreach and educational programmes, and to finance new exhibition initiatives and develop IT resources. In return the hubs must provide leadership and set new standards from which others can learn. They must continue to secure resources from public and private funds, the national lottery and not-for-profit organsiations. They must support the development of smaller and less well-funded institutions in their regions. As with New Labour's plans for distinguishing between specialist and so-called 'bog standard' comprehensive schools, we have to hope that these proposals do not advance the interests of the few at the expense of neglecting the majority.

3 / *The Contribution of Museums to the Inclusive Community: an Exploratory Study*[56], carried out by researchers at the universities of Newcastle and Stirling, also assesses the role of museums in fostering social inclusion. The two main aims of the study were (i) to provide empirical evidence to substantiate the claim that museums contribute to combatting social exclusion and (ii) to explore the ways in which museums can enable those labelled 'socially excluded' to negotiate their identities.

The researchers found that, whilst there is a belief among policy-makers in the social role of museums, there is little hard evidence to substantiate it. Their findings demonstrate that museums do have a role to play in fostering community development. However, their role is limited unless they are able to work in closer collaboration with other agencies.

They also found a lack of understanding amongst museum professionals about the incidence and causes of social exclusion. They found social inclusion to be widely equated with access and audience development, in the belief that social inclusion happens naturally once non-traditional visitors are persuaded through the doors. Because of the relatively slight attention paid to inter-agency consultation and collaboration, a somewhat isolationist approach to fostering social inclusion led to the potential of museums not being fully met. In this sense 'there is a lack of strategic direction in developing social inclusion initiatives in museums'.

On the other hand, the researchers acknowledge that museums have tended to be marginalised, particularly relative to sport and, to a lesser extent, the arts, in the social inclusion agenda. 'The absence of "hard deliverables" is the crucial factor here. Museums are clearly seen by policy makers as being a "good thing", though their agency role is blurred. Commensurately, they are encouraged, but largely under-funded in this role. The two initiatives (we studied in depth) were both funded by the Heritage

Lottery Fund rather than through core institutional funding'.

The researchers conclude that 'the ability of museums and galleries to socially engineer society, while an attractive idea to many museum workers, cannot at present be demonstrated'.[57]

IMPLICATIONS

The findings and recommendations expressed in all of these reports support the social impetus for change. The habitual users of arts organisations, libraries, archives, museums and galleries are revealed to be a relatively privileged and educationally successful section of the community, leaving enormous scope to increase and widen the appeal to other social groups. Clearly good work is being done but there is still a long way to go. All of the reports confirm that by increasing and diversifying participation, much more could be done to promote lifelong learning, to support personal, economic and social development and to help create a more cohesive and socially inclusive society. But all of those involved need to be much clearer about what it is they are being asked to do.

The incidence and causes of social exclusion are not sufficiently understood. There needs to be more collaboration across different agencies and providers. Serious consultation and on-going collaboration with non-traditional users and learners must be central to policy developments and initiatives. Evaluation exercises need to be qualitative, not simply quantitative. Social inclusion cannot be engineered, but socially-excluded groups should be supported in ways that respect their rights to participate in and benefit from the arts and cultural organisations which as citizens they own. With these wider social and economic aspirations in mind, more imaginative and committed leadership, more focused resources, more collaboration and partnership and a sea-change in institutional cultures, become urgent priorities.

In the present political climate, it is inevitable that arts and cultural organisations will find their public funding more closely tied to their willingness and capacity to support national policy priorities concerning lifelong learning, widening participation and social inclusion. But how they go should about doing it remains a matter of controversy.

[45] F Matarasso (1997) *Use or Ornament? The Social Impact of Participation in the Arts*, London: Comedia

[46] *Libraries for All: Social Inclusion in Public Libraries: Policy Guidance for Local Authorities in England*, DCMS 1999

[47] *Libraries, Museums, Galleries and Archives for All: Co-operating Across the Sectors to Tackle Social Exclusion*, DCMS 2001

[48] *Using Museums, Archives and Libraries to Develop a Learning Community: a Strategic Plan for Action: Draft for Consultation*, Resource 2001

[49] 2000

[50] 2000

[51] 2001 Policy Advisory Group First Report on Social Exclusion, Library Association

[52] P Roach and M Morrison (1998) Public Libraries, Ethnic Diversity and Citizenship, British Library Research and Innovation Report 76, University of Warwick

[53] 2000

[54] GLAMM Report p18

[55] GLAMM Report p17

[56] E Gilbert, A Newman, F McLean and G Urquhart (2001) *The Contribution of Museums to the Inclusive Community: An Exploratory Study*

[57] For further details of this research and future developments, please contact Andrew Newman, Department of Archaeology, University of Newcastle upon Tyne

6

CULTURAL EDUCATION FOR A CHANGE?

The expectation that art and culture should educate or ameliorate the human condition is not new and it remains contentious. According to Carol Duncan in *Civilizing Rituals, Inside Public Art Museums*,[58] there are three main views about the purpose of art museums. The aesthetic view holds that the serious pleasure of aesthetic contemplation has an inspirational value which needs no further justification. It is a view that was held by Kenneth Clark, the celebrated art historian, in his observation that 'the only reason for bringing together works of art in a public place is that...they produce in us a kind of exalted happiness. For a moment there is a clearing in the jungle; we pass on refreshed, with our capacity for life increased and with some memory of the sky'.[59] The second is the educational view, which is usually seen as being in opposition to the aesthetic, and which claims that art museums contribute to educating people aesthetically, visually, socially and historically. The third, political or ideological, view is that art museums are socially constructed institutions which carry out social and ideological functions in ways that reinforce dominant definitions of culture, knowledge and values and which co-opt visitors into becoming willing supporters of the status quo. 'Indeed, in the modern world, art museums constitute one of those sites in which politically organised and socially-institutionalised power most avidly seeks to realise its desire to appear as beautiful, natural and legitimate'.[60]

Art galleries, like museums and libraries, carry with them the legacy of nineteenth century aspirations about moral and social improvement and educational enlightenment for the deserving poor. In 1835, soon after the opening of the National Gallery in London, a Select Committee of the House of Commons was set up to consider the Government's involvement in art education and the management of public collections. Full of Benthamite reformers and radicals, the Committee spent considerable time debating ways to improve the taste of English artisans and designers in order to improve the design and competitiveness of British manufacturing.[61] The committee held the 'unshakeable belief that the very sight of art could improve the morals and deportment of even the lowest social ranks'.[62] In similar vein, Charles Dickens, speaking in 1852 at the opening of Manchester Public Library, claimed that the library would provide a 'source of pleasure and improvement in the cottages, the garrets and the ghettos of the poorest of our people'.[63]

But the educative and inclusive nature of this heritage proved to be both superficial and short-lived. Victorian libraries and museums concentrated on the deserving poor and drew the line at criminals, vagrants and those resident in the poorhouse. Library rules enforcing clean hands and faces were often rigorously imposed to counteract fears about the transmission of disease and contagion through books. And although they were initially intended to improve and educate the masses, both libraries and museums were soon taken over by the middle-class in ways that continue to affect their present cultures and clientèle.[64] By the end of the nineteenth century, the educators and improvers had been effectively marginalised and the aesthetes were in the ascendancy. It is a focus that has not gone away, although increasing the demand for arts and cultural learning is now back on the political and cultural agenda, especially in relation to non-traditional audiences.

CULTURAL POLITICS

Whether or not museums, or indeed culture, can be regarded as political is a question addressed by Richard Hoggart in the British Museum's Second Annual Franks Lecture in 1998.[65]

Echoing Raymond Williams, his argument assumes an organic relationship between museums-as-sites and the self-perceptions of different national cultures. Because culture is at the heart of every nation's sense of itself, and if the aim is to have in New Labour's language an inclusive or cohesive society, it is important 'to pay great attention to cultural elements'.[66] Decisions about how culture is represented reflect deeper judgements based on power and authority. Cultural selections are used to make claims about what a nation is or ought to be, as well as how citizens should relate to each other. None of this is neutral territory.

Like Williams, Hoggart is a democrat and an adult educator. He believes that a decent society must give all its members the opportunity to open their minds to what are generally regarded as the best kinds of creativity and the best works of the intellect and imagination. Through democratising knowledge, a society can begin to mature:

> A society which does not recognise this imperative will be populated by well-fed morons, not by cultivated humans. Of course, if anyone settles for being a plump moron, one cannot forbid them; but they should have the opportunity to realise what they are missing'.[67]

To satisfy this altogether larger hunger, people need both access and education.

In terms of audiences, Hoggart quotes a nineteenth century Bishop and an eighteenth century playwright to support his insistence that cultural education must reach beyond existing audiences because 'the number of people who need to be awakened is far greater than those who need comfort' and 'we must not accept the wantlessness of the poor'. He warns cultural workers not to take

> present audiences as sufficient guide to potential others; do not half consciously assign some people to previously class-and-education bound slots; do not underestimate the capacities of many thousands outside. Only the best is good enough for anyone else, as we assume it is for us and our kind.[68]

This is an argument for making what is currently available to the few, more widely accessible to all. It is not an argument for making life easy. In terms of popularising culture it means offering people not simply the things they already like but also the things they do not know they will like until they have experience of them. It does not mean 'giving the people what they want' or 'what some powers-that-be want to ram down their throats for their own purposes' – it means offering very much more and it means 'taking a gamble' on our own and our fellow citizens' possibilities. In Hoggart's view,

> a would-be civilised democracy will not abuse culture for immediate political ends, nor impose its own pre-determined definition of culture on its people. It will be open, democratic, not bullying

nor endlessly all-things-to-all-men-or-women. It will offer perspectives on the better and the best; its citizens will be free to be both inside and outside their own cultural overcoats.[69]

But if Carol Duncan's analysis is correct, the possibility of a more democratic, better educated and socially inclusive society poses a serious challenge to what art and cultural institutions are actually for and about how they operate. Duncan's recognition of the political nature of art museums is that they carry out social and ideological functions in ways that reinforce the status quo. What she has to say is also relevant to museums more generally as well as libraries, theatres and concert halls. She is quite clear that art museums are not the 'neutral and transparent sheltering places for objects' which they are often claimed to be. They are better understood as sites of cultural activity which offer up partisan values and beliefs about social, sexual and political identity.

It is a view shared by the Guerilla Girls, a group of western women artists and arts professionals fighting discrimination in the art world. They show how the history of western art has been a history of discrimination. Their question is not 'Why haven't there been more great women artists?' but rather 'Why haven't more women been considered great artists?' Not only is the existence of women artists largely hidden from history but also women continue to get collected less and shown less. Museums and galleries in Europe and New York are least available to women. In a wonderfully subversive poster campaign, the Guerilla Girls pose the question 'Do women have to be naked to get into the Metropolitan Museum of Modern Art?' Apparently they do. Less than 5 per cent of the artists in the modern art sections are women but 85 per cent of the nudes on show are female.[70]

The Arts Council for England, in preparing to update its Cultural Diversity policy for the period 2002-7, also takes as its starting point the evidence of prejudice and discrimination in the arts world, in this case against minorities, for example:

- a straw poll taken in 1999 found 177 Black, Asian and Chinese employees in 2,900 employees in 18 Arts Council-funded venues. Out of those, one was in upper management and 100 were in catering.

- audiences for major mainstream arts venues consistently fail to reflect the demography of the urban areas in which they are sited. One in five of London's inhabitants comes from minority ethnic communities. One eighth of all people from minority ethnic communities live in the West Midlands. These proportions are not to be found among the audiences for major mainstream cultural venues.

- black, Asian and Chinese arts initiatives, coming from a narrower base, were disproportionately weakened during the 1980s recession and still do not enjoy parity in terms of funding. Under the first Capital Lottery programme, only 0.2 per cent of the funds disbursed went to black, Asian or Chinese projects. Broadly this was firstly because of a criterion that militated against black, Asian and Chinese ventures and, secondly, because of cynicism and alienation in that sector.

- the economics of vocational arts training courses and local authorities' discretionary schemes act against ethnic minority students. Seventy per cent of England's people from ethnic minorities live in 88 of the most deprived local authority areas. It is therefore unlikely that they will be able to take advantage of discretionary grants or indeed have access to quality arts in their area.

- a small handful of centres or venues are run or led by black, Asian or Chinese-led groups. In general, smaller centres form valuable grassroots training grounds for future administrators and artists, 'safe houses' where young people can cut their artistic teeth. Historically, such black-led venues as have existed have been based in deprived areas to which European funds have been targeted (eg Drum in Birmingham, Nia in Manchester). This has loaded the scales against the venture from the start since disadvantaged areas lack a strong arts-going public. This has been frequently compounded by poor local infrastructure and transport links.

- there is considerable (indeed, growing) misunderstanding around 'multiculturalism', its character and function. Tensions over refugees and asylum-seekers have tended to portray diversity as a dangerous dilution to national identity.

- the debate over 'cultural diversity' has become trapped in hostile visions of racial separation, unfairly favoured minorities and a terminally divided society. It has also been affected by re-configurations of national identity encouraged by the establishment of a national parliament in Scotland and a national assembly in Wales, wavering moves towards Europe, and economic and cultural globalisation. Cultural theorists such as Stuart Hall and Sarat Maharaj have spoken up for the new Britain, but it needs more passionate advocates in arts policy.

Of equal concern are the ways in which western museums represent foreign cultures: how their displays of 'primitive', 'third world' or non-western artifacts often misrepresent or re-invent other cultures, for what are ultimately ideological purposes. The issues relating to what western museums do to foreign cultures, including the minority cultures within their own societies, are especially urgent as post-colonial societies try to define and redefine their cultural identities and as minority cultures in the West seek cultural recognition.

It is not only feminists and members of minority cultures who point out that what counts as art is a reflection of historical selection and social and political power. In what is an otherwise sober commentary from researchers at Leicester University, there comes the observation that 'for a long time museums have reflected a society largely white, middle-class, male, imperialist, straight and dead.'[71] Clearly these are representations which are changing, and they no longer go unchallenged, but not sufficiently, it seems, to make the writers' comment irrelevant.

Carol Duncan makes a rather different point about the social and ideological function of art museums. She describes art museums (and similar observations could be made about libraries, concert halls and theatres) as ritual spaces, marked-off in time and place from people's ordinary concerns and ordinary lives, to which they come to engage in a different quality of experience. The experience involves them in rituals appropriate to the setting, which they perform rather like a script or a score. They may witness

a drama or hear a recital of texts or special music. They may enact a performance themselves, often individually and alone, by following a pre-
scribed route or observing appropriate decorum. Some may use ritual
sites more knowledgeably than others; they may be more culturally attuned
to their symbolic cues.

Pierre Bourdieu has also described how some are more equal than others
when it comes to performing these rituals and why a visit to an art museum
gives some people the feeling of cultural ownership and belonging whilst
others feel inferior and excluded. This is partly, but not entirely, to do with
cultural capital.[72]

Cultural capital is not related to intelligence or ability but is more about
the knowledge and know-how required to progress through the system
and about knowing how the system works. It is partly as a consequence of
having the appropriate cultural capital that white upper middle-class identities and privileges are able to flourish despite the alleged demise of
social class distinctions in this society and the growth of multiculturalism.
In relation to the arts – including painting, music, theatre and literature –
an important ingredient of 'the right' cultural capital is the way in which
middle-class and upper middle-class children are more likely than
working-class children to inherit a love of these pursuits. Not only does this
give them a familiarity with the 'great masters' of European culture, which
is in itself an indication of belonging to a social elite, but it enables them
to function appropriately in relation to their work. Put simply, those with
the right kinds of cultural capital are more at ease in galleries and concert
halls, they know how to behave when they are in them, and through their
presence, they help actively to re-constitute what galleries and concert
halls represent.

Duncan adds an important corollary to this view, in that those who are best
prepared to perform museum rituals, 'those who are most able to respond
to its various cues are also those whose identities (social, sexual, racial)
the museum ritual most fully confirms'.[73] In other words, 'what we see and
do not see in art museums – and on what terms and by whose authority
we do or do not see it – is closely linked to larger questions about who constitutes the community and who shall exercise the power to define its
identity'.[74] In this way, art museums act to reinforce prevailing power and

authority systems that are closely associated with social divisions and social inequalities. That is what they are there for. It is also the reason why their social purpose and cultural practices need to be contested and why proposed changes are fiercely debated.

CULTURAL SNIPINGS

Mark O'Neill, head of museums and galleries at Glasgow City Council, provides a vivid insight into one such debate that has been taking place in Glasgow.[75] He describes a number of exhibitions which experimented in 'a fairly mild way' with the content, display and interpretation of art in the city's galleries throughout the 1990s and the 'extremely hostile' criticism which this evoked. Quoting from the critics' reviews, which are full of sound and fury, he finds plenty of evidence of the passion and intensity which are a symptom of a group experiencing change as an attack. His analysis of the underlying assumptions of the critics makes brilliant and perceptive reading. For example, whilst the critics are clearly angry with the curators responsible for these exhibitions, their attack is focussed on the intended audience.

> All the critics strongly imply that anyone who enjoyed these exhibitions is somehow not a good enough person to be in an art gallery. If they liked the videos and the costume and the theatricality of the Birth of Impressionism, if they thought the shipyard sets were evocative, if they found St Mungo's inspiring, if they thought the eclectic mix in Glasgow's Gallery of Modern Art exciting, then they are punters, they can't take their art neat, they are shoppers or voyeurs in a pornography shop, they have a mental age of four, and are so weak-minded that they might be damaged by the exhibition; they are the kind of ghouls who would enjoy public executions. This kind of exhibition, the critics say, is no longer for us, who belong here, but for *them*, who don't.[76]

The critical reviews of the Glasgow exhibitions are symptomatic of more general criticisms made of art galleries and museums (and universities) which attempt to be socially inclusive. The most common charge is of superficiality, of dumbing-down: 'This is leveled at exhibitions which provide basic information, for example, especially if it is done using a format which is different from (usual conventions)... Most art museums...provide virtually no information about the exhibits for visitors. How can it be superficial to provide more information?'[77]

Another charge is that art and culture in the modern age has moved away from anything difficult, that there is a pretence that everything can be made easy. O'Neill quite rightly reminds those, who romanticise a former, golden age, that there has only ever been a tiny minority of the population sufficiently privileged through wealth and leisure to seek out subjects of intellectual difficulty. The question of cultural growth, as Raymond Williams argues, needs 'full space' for difficulty and 'full time' for originality so that it is not just a continuation of 'old rules'. In Richard Hoggart's words, all people should have the opportunity to 'open their minds to the best kinds of creativity', to the best works of 'the intellect and imagination'. In O'Neill's opinion, 'It is mean-minded (to imply) that people whose life opportunities have been limited by poverty, illness, poor education and discrimination, have to undergo some sort of painful initiation, to earn the right to basic information about what they as citizens own'.[78]

CHANGING PLACES

The Arts Council has agreed a definition of social exclusion which takes low income as its starting point and focuses particularly on poverty in combination with other factors, such as low educational attainment, poor health, crime and unemployment. This is sufficient to meet the Government's priorities in relation to neighbourhood renewal. Parallel strategies in relation to disability and diversity are also in place.

As far as diversity is concerned, the Council's intention is to 'celebrate diversity and create ongoing support for black and Asian artists, managers and audiences'. This involves a definition of diversity in relation to specific racial groups which others might find restricted. The Diversity Council, for example, which is a network of library and information workers, has developed a much broader (and some would say, more inclusive) definition of diversity. As well as race, religion, culture and ethnicity, it also covers social class, gender and sexuality, and includes refugees and asylum-seekers, homeless people and travelers, housebound people, disabled people, unemployed people and prisoners and their families.

To go beyond the limited obligation to provide physical access to previously excluded groups, in ways that also provide cultural, emotional and intellectual access to the meaning and understanding of art and culture, requires fundamental changes to take place in the assumptions and conventions of arts and cultural organisations. It also requires fundamental changes in public perceptions and expectations about what we think arts and culture organisations ought to provide as a measure of cultural democracy.

In *Renaissance in the Regions*, the report writers discovered poorly managed museums and galleries that reflected a generation of neglect by politicians and policy-makers. The report called for a strategic approach to revitalising the role of regional museums and galleries as a contribution to government regional and regeneration agendas and to maximising their potential for education and social inclusion.[79]

In similar vein, *Open to All?*[80] identified a conservative profession with managers ill-informed about the issues involved and reluctant to change. The core conclusion of the study was that whilst public libraries have the potential to play a key role in tackling social exclusion, in order to make a real difference they need to undergo rapid transformation and change.

Although change is widely called for, it is not necessarily welcomed or fully understood. The Arts Council, for example, in its response to the Government's social exclusion agenda appears somewhat cautious. The Council is quick to defend its record, or at least the record of those artists who have 'always worked within the context of what is currently termed "social exclusion" many (of whom) have had a life-changing effect on those with whom they work (and whose) work the Arts Council wishes to recognise and enhance.'[81] But it is also keen to point out that 'to set out to use the arts for instrumental purposes only is to undermine artists' work'. This is a claim made in defense of artistic freedom and integrity and an understandable scepticism about being cajoled into delivering New Labour's enthusiasm for social engineering when it comes to those who are socially excluded. The Council is reluctant to require all of its regularly funded bodies to be committed to work with socially excluded groups. For some, the Council thinks, such a requirement would be inappropriate. In other respects, there is a reluctance to compromise the work of organisations that are making distinctive contributions in this area, at least not until a lot more is known about appropriate provision and evaluating its impact.

These are all reservations which merit consideration but they are also reminiscent of what Raymond Williams used to call the 'leave me alone I'm an artist tendency'. He condemned 'abstract and impossible' notions of artistic freedom in favour of making an historical or social alignment which not only gives the artist a voice *as* itself but also for *more than* itself. Artistic freedom is a position that might easily be read as a reluctance to change, in ways that could be construed as elitist.

The Arts Council is not alone in its reluctance to be drawn into social and political agendas. Librarians and curators frequently complain that they are not therapists or social workers, they cannot be expected to compensate for the inadequacies of the state education system or an ill-divided society. Neither is the welfare approach to cultural provision, which adds on a few projects and activities for the regularly excluded, to appease political pressures and social consciences, likely to make much difference to social inequality. The business of targeting specific groups as a way of addressing exclusion may actually increase the competition between disadvantaged groups for scarce resources and serve to penalise 'less fashionable' groups as well as reinforcing social and cultural differences, rather than encouraging mutual respect and recognition.

For all of these and other reasons, equal opportunities need to be at the heart of arts and cultural strategies to open up access and invite wider participation, rather than be added on as an optional extra. And organisations who are not actively involved in removing the barriers to what they have to offer should be held to account for effectively reinforcing them. 'If social inclusion means anything, it means actively seeking out and removing barriers, of acknowledging that people who have been left out for generations need additional support in a whole variety of ways to enable them to exercise their rights to participate in many of the facilities which the better off and better educated take for granted.'[82]

In the case of art museums, Mark O'Neill asks whether the reluctance to change is 'designed to protect a valued tradition which is coincidentally and not intentionally exclusive? Or is it that art museums, as currently conceived, are inherently exclusive?'[83] Like Williams, he is concerned with questions of social justice and political responsibility. 'Given the value of our tradition, should we be the last to change? Given the value of what we can offer, should we be in the forefront of creating equality?' In Glasgow, at least, the answer seems to be in favour of making equality a high priority, in ways that mean:

- accepting the level of education of potential visitors as they are as the starting point

- accepting that many of the conventions of museums are traditions valued by many but which may need to be modified to be welcoming to new visitors

- that museum staff can only understand the reality of exclusion by working with representatives of excluding groups

- that a pluralistic approach must be developed to displays so that everyone from the novice to the scholar feels welcome

- redefining research, so that the staff are as informed and as rigorous about visitors as about collections

- redefining display standards so that they not only look beautiful, but also provide access, in all senses, to diverse audiences, in ways that respect the realities of their lives

[58] C Duncan (1995) *Civilizing Rituals, Inside Public Art Museums*, London: Routledge

[59] K Clark (1954) 'The Ideal Museum', *ArtNews*, January 1954, vol 52, p.29

[60] Duncan *op cit* p. 6

[61] M O'Neill, 'The Good Enough Visitor' in (2002) *Museums, Society, Inequality* (ed) Richard Sandall, London: Routledge

[62] Duncan *op cit* p 42/3

[63] D Muddiman *et al* (2000) *Open to All? The Public Library and Social Exclusion*, Resource

[64] 5 per cent of the population make half the annual visits to museums and galleries. 30 per cent of the population are library users, two out of three of whom are middle-class. There are no national figures to indicate the use made of libraries and museums by minority ethnic communities although it is known that black and minority ethnic staff comprise only 2 per cent of staff in libraries and 2.2 per cent of

museums' and galleries' total workforce – the majority of whom are guards and catering staff.

[65] R Hoggart (2001) 'Are Museums Political' in *Between Two Worlds: Essays*, London: Arum Press

[66] *ibid* p 12

[67] R Hoggart (2001) 'Literacy is not Enough' in *Between Two Worlds: Essays*, London: Arum Press

[68] *op cit* p15

[69] *ibid* p17

[70] The Guerilla Girls (1998) *The Guerilla Girls Bedside Companion to the History of Western Art*, Harmondsworth: Penguin

[71] (2000) *Museums and Social Inclusion; The GLAMM Report* p 17 Leicester University

[72] P Bourdieu *et al* (1991) *The Love of Art: European Art Museums and their Public*, Cambridge. Originally written in 1969

[73] Duncan *op cit* p6

[74] *ibid* p6

[75] O'Neill *op cit*

[76] *ibid*

[77] *ibid*

[78] *ibid*

[79] DCMS (2001) *Renaissance in the Regions: A New Vision for England's Museums*

[80] D Muddiman *et al* (2000) *Open to All? The Public Library and Social Exclusion*, Resource

[81] Arts Council of England, update on the Council's response to PAT 10

[82] M O'Neill *op cit*

[83] *ibid*

THE TILBURY B
BAND — FOUN
1919 BY THE
BRANCH OF TH
NATIONAL UNIO
RAILWAYMEN A
STILL ACTIVELY
PROMOTING TH
BRASS BAND
MOVEMENT BY
GIVING FREE
LESSONS
AND LOANING
INSTRUMENTS
THOSE WHO N
THEM.

P A R T

THREE

*Consuming
Passions*

7
INSPIRATIONS

What is missing from this discussion so far are the voices of those involved in arts and cultural learning and some examples of the kinds of activities that are turning people on to active engagement in arts and culture. I include here some of my favourite inspirations to give a sense of what is happening and what is possible. There are clearly many, many others that could have been included.

ALL THE WORLD'S A STAGE

'All the world's a stage,' announces the Globe Theatre's tour and exhibition promotion on London's South Bank. And when you take the tour, you are soon reminded that, in Shakespeare's day at least, the Globe was an authentic and popular theatre for the people.

Just a stone's throw away on the breeze-block walls of a shared office space, underneath a block of flats, a makeshift gallery of compelling images catches the magic of ordinary people transformed by the pleasure of performance into dancers, actors and story tellers. 1st Framework was set up by director/designer Peter Avery and producer Maxine Webster in 1982 to bring together arts practitioners and community groups in unconventional venues, to work together on musical and theatrical productions that are both challenging and experiential. As part of the Voluntary Arts Network, 1st Framework – with its mix of artists, volunteers and local groups – is making an important contribution to realising the cultural and creative potential of lifelong learning.

Over 100 years earlier, Mary Ward achieved modest fame in her own lifetime as a best-selling novelist, but she has had a more enduring impact on public education through the pioneering work she initiated at the settlement she founded which now bears her name. On the agenda was a rich mix of clubs, concerts, debates and lectures that reached the lives of ordinary people. Her declared aim was to promote 'equalisation' in society and the settlement was soon crammed with local residents enjoying 'the hundreds of pleasures and opportunities that fall mainly to the rich'. Concerts and music were always an important part of the programme. The building acted as a magnet to local people who came to develop intellectual pursuits and learn practical skills, but also to be part of a social and community network that included groups interested in music and debating, and self-help groups like the Coal Club and the Poor Man's Lawyer Service. At the turn of the century, George Bernard Shaw, Sydney Webb and Keir Hardie lived in the settlement's bachelor accommodation and gave lectures about how best to create a more equal and just society.

Today the Mary Ward Centre still takes the values and priorities of its founder seriously and continues to be a place for ideals and enthusiasm. It is no surprise, therefore, that some of the Centre's current members have become energetic partners with 1st Framework in a number of community arts initiatives in recent years. The Over-60s Drama Group, for instance, is keen to encourage older people to 'lay claim to their futures in diverse and creative ways' and 'to challenge the historical stereotype that older people are reluctant to embrace new ideas'. Besides local performances, they have now toured their performances to schools, community centres and residential homes throughout the UK, and most recently, to Australia. In 1996 the partnership won first prize for their production of Stories in Ireland during the European Year of Lifelong Learning. Georgina Dobson, who took the role of Ariel in a production of *The Tempest* at the Edinburgh Festival, now entertains most Tuesday nights at a gay bar in Mayfair. According to Maxine, 'a cab comes to collect her on cabaret night almost every week. She has a great singing voice and the songs she likes to sing seem to go down very well'.

On tour in 2000 with Green Candle Dance Company, 1st Framework took their 'join-in-the-production-approach' to community arts to five different regions across the country. Starting with a skeleton script, describing simple and abstract visual ideas of 'home', and a core professional company of dancers, musicians, designers and technical crew, they stayed in each location for ten days. Working together with a rich mix of local arts organisations, schools, colleges, community groups, brass bands, dance groups, special needs centres, asylum-seekers, community choirs and older people they were able to build up a production that was unique to each place. The final show was presented as a promenade performance, with different groups contributing to different scenes, before an exuberant finale brought everyone involved to their feet, dancing to music played by a brass band. Maxine reports that 'in Sandwell and Dudley we had a terrific time. We made contact with local voluntary and community groups through Sandwell Social Services and Black Country Touring … providing ideas and raising issues we would never have thought up for ourselves'. Not only did local groups get a lot of pleasure from taking part in the Home project, but also the workshop format allowed for significant and difficult issues to be explored creatively through the inter-play of improvisation, music, theatre and dance.

In an effort to sustain this type of community learning, 1st Framework is now helping the groups they have come into contact with to make their own websites, with hyperlinks to strengthen the contacts between them. Another partnership – this time with Community Action Network and the Rural Development Agency – has provided training and support for the groups involved, with computer hardware supplied by Sainsbury's. The websites came in very useful to develop projects to link in with 2001 – the International Year of The Volunteer.

'We're learning all the time', says Peter. 'Although it's easy enough to make sure that people enjoy themselves and have a good time, we do set high standards and take a few risks …in the interests of stretching people's imagination and increasing their sense of achievement'.

1st Framework's latest project involves musicians from English National Opera's Baylis Programme and a cast of local people from Southwark to stage Bertolt Brecht's *Threepenny Opera*. The idea came during an exchange visit between The Mary Ward Over Sixties Group and social work students from Berlin to celebrate the International Year of Older People in 1999. The production provides employment for a promising group of young people in the creative industries, participation for older people as performers and singers and volunteering opportunities for artists and various well-wishers.

The preparations for the performances began with workshops to give everyone involved a sense of the period and what Brecht had a mind. This included the study of an original film version of the opera made by Pabst in

Berlin in 1922. The score contains original material just recently released by the Kurt Weill Institute in New York. Already the production has played to enthusiastic audiences in Tower Hamlets, Croydon and Southwark, in locations chosen for their resonance with Mac the Knife's London. The project ends its tour in 2002 in Berlin, in the famous former German film studio where Pabst made the original film version of the opera. The studios are now an Adult Education Institute and Housing Co-op called UFA Fabrik, based on radical ideas about sustainable development and citizenship education.

According to Maxine, raising money for projects like this is relentless. Funding bodies don't always allow for 'joined up' initiatives across separate and different organisations – on a local, national and inter-national scale. Not everyone agrees that encouraging people to work on creative projects together is 'educational in itself' although the opportunities to learn about other peoples lives and to swap information and experience is invaluable. 'Sometimes we get payment in kind. For example, Japan Airlines gave us a big reduction on our Australian tickets. Sometimes we get free use of a venue to stage the final performance, or the free use of a couple of rooms big enough to hold the workshops in. When we took the Home Project to the Midlands, all the volunteers and artists were fed each lunch time by the Bangladeshi Women's group who were one of the groups taking part in the project'.

But no one who has seen the enthusiasm and mutual learning generated by this kind of work could be in any doubt about its value and importance. It is just the kind of antidote that is needed to rescue ordinary people – especially those in deprived communities and groups – from the worst excesses of current policy directives, which too often seem preoccupied with either reforming or reprimanding the socially excluded in the name of neighbourhood renewal.

Mary Ward was right. In the struggle to promote 'equalisation' in society – or in today's language, 'greater equity and social justice' – those who are poor still need to share in the 'hundreds of pleasures and opportunities that fall mainly to the rich'. Whilst present Government policies to widen participation in education, combat social exclusion and re-generate communities are primarily intended to promote learning and skills and to bridge the widening gap between rich and poor – it is important to remember that community arts can help to get in touch with the places that 'straight' policy and 'formal' educational initiatives often fail to reach.

For further details contact the 1st Framework website: www.1stframework.org.uk

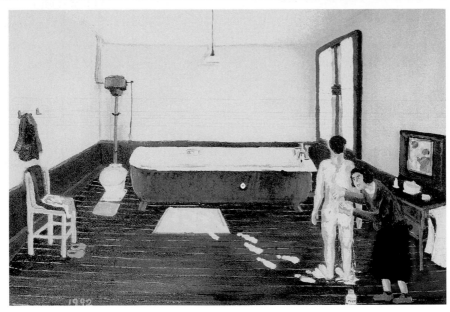

THE PAINTED BATH

AT MRS ALES'S, THE BATH WAS COVERED IN RUST SPOTS. ONCE MRS ALES THOUGHT SHE WOULD MAKE THE BATHROOM LOOK NICER BY PAINTING THE BATH. SHE TOLD ME NOT TO USE IT FOR A WEEK.

AFTER A WEEK I HAD A BATH, NICE HOT WATER AND PLENTY OF SOAP. WHEN I GOT OUT, I NOTICED THESE WHITE FOOTPRINTS ON THE FLOOR. MY FEET WERE WHITE. THEN I SAW IN THE MIRROR MY LEGS, BOTTOM AND BACK WERE ALL WHITE TOO — WET PAINT.

HERE'S DORIS CLEANING ME OFF WITH TURPENTINE. DORIS IS LAUGHING, BUT I'M FURIOUS — 'THAT STUPID BLOODY WOMAN!' — AND THAT'S MAKING DORIS LAUGH ALL THE MORE.

FUNNY OLD THING MRS ALES WAS — EVERY THURSDAY SHE WOULD COME TO COLLECT THE RENT, BUT SHE NEVER CAME IN, JUST STOOD OUTSIDE THE DOOR AND COUGHED UNTIL I PAID HER.

Mr F.S. Smith
Kings Heath
Birmingham

Dear Jane,

I Frank Sidney Smith become an artist an author by going to night school classes for over 20 years. Born in the Workhouse and in a childrens home, that life left me with sad memries. Then life in war time and army life and married life, sad in places. But doing my paintings and writing a life auto-biography is a great challeng to write. I had the help in my spelling by going to night school. I have to thank all education teachers and volunteers that have done their part.

But theres more I am doing this very day. That is sculpture in clay! This will be much harder than ever at the end. Im out to do a A leavle of a teenage boy of me. Little Frank Then a bronze that is my ambition. I know I can do it.

Im writing some books to go with all shown in the paintings and sculpture - to put all the stories that go with each one I do and Im well on the way. I have an exhibition too that took all most four years to make. I donot think there is an artist that has took on his life of 72 years of this true life story and can proov they are all true.

F.S. Smith

RESTING AT DINNER TIME

SINCE I DIDN'T GET MUCH SLEEP AT NIGHT, I OFTEN TOOK A NAP DURING MY BREAKS AT WORK. HERE I AM IN MY CORNER.

I SLEPT DEEPLY DURING THE BREAKS. THE OTHERS SOMETIMES PLAYED TRICKS ON ME. ONCE THEY TIED MY BOOTS TOGETHER. WHEN I WOKE UP, I STOOD UP AND FELL OVER. ANOTHER TIME, WHEN I WAS SNORING, SOMEONE DROPPED A TIN JUST BY ME, MAKING ME JUMP OUT OF MY SKIN.

SOON AFTER DORIS'S DEATH I WAS MADE REDUNDANT BECAUSE THE PLACE WAS TOO NOISY. I HAD BEEN SENSITIVE TO NOISE EVER SINCE THE NAVAL GUNS DAMAGED MY EARDRUMS.

NOT LONG AFTER, THE PERCY ROAD WORKS WERE BULLDOZED. IT'S ALL FLAT CONCRETE NOW.

London Voices was the theme for the 2001 Workers' Educational Association (WEA) London District's poetry competition which attracted contributions from WEA creative writing groups, women's groups and local art history and history groups. The winning entry came from Kathleen Miles from the Sidcup WEA creative writing group.

CITY MISTS

The river flows
below layered
blankets of fog.
New buildings hide
beneath plastic
wraps in bleak sky.
Tower blocks high
a chairman sits
surrounded by
blue cigar smoke,
remembering his
boyhood winters,
when diamond webs
hung in hedgerows
and horses heads
rose like unveiled
statues from white
curtains of mist.
Soon he will speak
to shareholders,
blurring issues
with obscure words,
which will spread,
through the city
like turbulent clouds,
making profits from murky deals,
as hazy sun
hangs useless on
the horizon.

In terms of serious cool, it's hard to top Beat Dis. Run by a group of black jazz musicians from a community centre tucked away in a quiet Notting Hill square, Beat Dis is more than a music workshop, it is more even than a local internet radio station. It is a way of life.

From offices and studios rented from The Tabernacle, a lottery-funded arts centre, Beat Dis has started training people from the local community as programme editors, sound mixers, journalists, presenters, administrators – whatever they want to be. The training is hands-on and it is real. These are not pretend jobs and they are not pretend opportunities. Project leader Tony Thomas asserts: "It would cost you £500 in the private sector to buy the kind of training we're offering. If you look at who's providing courses for the young and unemployed then we're putting most Government-run organisations to shame. We're a bunch of musicians with degrees – but I'd challenge anyone to produce the results we have on the budget we've got."

The BBC's community radio London Live's partnership in the Beat Dis internet radio project is an important boost. The community and the trainees are setting the agenda for this station and there are programme slots for local news stories, history, rap music, schools and colleges, and of course the world-famous Notting Hill Carnival. It is the authentic voice of a very diverse and vibrant community and the BBC is keen to tap into it. Which is why the BBC is also installing two-way TV and sound recording equipment to boost Beat Dis' already impressive state-of-the-art technology.

Santana recently played a little-publicised gig at The Tabernacle and soon shows like this will be simultaneously recorded and transmitted live on the internet. Journalism is also part of the package of creating community radio and on the afternoon I visited, BBC radio journalist Sian Lord was leading a training session on interview techniques – keeping celebrities or politicians to the point, and getting that all-important sound bite without resorting to trickery. Around 20 Beat Dis trainees, many of whom will soon be on the streets with digital audio recorders, were bombarding her with questions.

For trainee Jimmy Sydney (33) work at Beat Dis is rescuing him from a
series of dead-end jobs managing bars and restaurants. He wants to get
out there and DJ. "I left school at 15 and for me the internet training is
boosting my employability and confidence. We work as a team and Tony
gets a lot of respect."

Come the Carnival Beat Dis will be live on air. The hours of training in sound mixing and journalism and the many other skills will soon pay off. As Tony says, his philosophy is to take on people for their enthusiasm, to train them and to help them learn from each other. It costs a lot of money to run an outfit like this and Tony has no time for people who sit in committees and debate whether they can afford this or that piece of kit. If the equipment is cutting edge and it is available then Beat Dis has to have it. Tony says: "What we don't do is train people on equipment that is two or three years old and then send them out to try and get work. The sound studios round here would just turn round and laugh at us. 'What? You don't know this?? It's industry standard!'" Catch them on www.portobello2000.co.uk!

Information supplied by NIACE Adult and Community Learning Fund which has helped to fund Beat Dis

So said Emma Goldman, the American campaigner for personal freedom and social justice 'if I can't dance, I won't join your revolution'. She was always acute in her criticisms of both contemporary Russian and American society and vociferous in her opinions 'I may be arrested, I may be tied and thrown into jail, but I will never be silent...' but she understood profoundly about the human spirit and its need to flourish.

✺ **DANCING NATION** is a video produced by the Foundation for Community Dance to record examples of people dancing in their different communities in the year 2000, and to offer inspiration and advice to others in the public and voluntary sectors who may want to include dance in their activities. Each year in England alone around 4 million people take part in community dance activities every week, initiated by dance professionals, companies and agencies. The dance sector reaches out beyond the boundaries of theatres and arts centres to the places where people live and has an impressive record of providing accessible and relevant opportunities irrespective of age, ability, social or economic background

STILL FROM
THE FILM
DANCING NATION BY
ROSEMARY LEE AND
PETER ANDERSON

COMMISSIONED AND
PRODUCED BY THE
FOUNDATION FOR
COMMUNITY DANCE

Dance can be about many things: meeting people, staying fit, having fun, relaxing – but it is also about so much more than this. Dance enables people to explore and find creativity for themselves and in themselves, to share new physical languages, to become artists for a moment or more, and to feel a well-being in their whole body. Dance can also be an equaliser – it has the capacity to engage people of all abilities and to encourage them to be communally creative and original. There are wonderful moments when the dancer is so at one with the activity, so comfortable, so unselfconscious – that dance fills their every sinew and breath. These are, in their own way, transformative moments.

COMMUNITY DANCE IS ABOUT:

- dance that engages directly with people as they define themselves; valuing and respecting who they are, their differences and what they bring individually and collectively to that engagement

- experiences that contribute positively to self-worth, self-confidence and a sense of well-being

- experiences that are achievable – yet testing, over which they have a sense of ownership, control and belonging

- a framework for learning and making effective use of artform skills

- providing sustained support that allows people to grow, develop, gain a sense of achievement and make a contribution within their wider communities

- engaging people creatively in solving problems, seeking solutions, finding a form that expresses their concerns, cultures and aspirations as well as thinking critically about their experience

- providing opportunities for people to develop more positive and active relationships with their wider communities

✸ **STREET BEAT** was launched in 1998 for boys and young men aged 8-13 and 12-22 in Warrington. It is funded by the Cultural Development Service of Warrington Borough Council. Street Beat teaches breakdance and gives young men a chance to excel and develop their skills within a 'lads-only' environment. Breakdance is an inclusive artform. It engages with each person's personality and encourages camaraderie and equality.

Popping, breaking, power moves, intricate footwork painstakingly perfected all represent something of the dancer and become like a visible voice.

Street Beat builds on the lads' existing culture – the language, clothes, music and attitude are all an integral part of the performance. There's an exhibitionism about breaking and a competitive edge that clearly appeals to the young men. The dancing takes skill and their passion for improving comes from their total comfort with the dance form and the dedicated structure of the teaching sessions.

Breaking is a dialogue, a call and response between individual dancers, crews and the audience – it connects them. Crews challenge each other to the dance but it is common to find them helping less experienced breakers. Choreography is done democratically and there exists a sense of ownership. The ethos that drives Street Beat is respect, good attitude and hard graft. Bad language, poor attitudes and unhealthy competition are not tolerated. Young men tend to be incredibly territorial but in this group it seems that lads from very different areas bond together with the common aim of improving their dance.

❋ **AMICI DANCE THEATRE** was launched in 1980 as a performing company of both large and small scale productions and is based at the Sand End Centre in Fulham. When AMICI started it was the first company in Britain to include people with disabilities in public dance performances. The work focuses on the skills of dance and performance rather than therapy. The philosophy of AMICI is that people can dance together regardless of their backgrounds or abilities – indeed the very concept of disability is challenged. The company's director choreographs most of the large-scale productions but AMICI encourages its members to create pieces for the company. Its current repertoire includes works devised by blind members and people with learning difficulties – thus pioneering the development and presentation of the choreographic skills of disabled people.

❋ **DUG OUT** adult community dance company was launched in 1990 and is funded by East and South Oxford Community Education. Dug Out has evolved an inclusive and collaborative approach which integrates everyone's work in a respectful and supportive way. Dancers are aged between 20 and 82 and come from all kinds of different backgrounds. They learn about dance as an artform and also become skilled as technicians, improvisers, in partnering, contact and choreographic methods. High levels of artistic integrity are expected and all the performances and workshops involve considerable reflection and evaluation. The company is a testament to what can be achieved when committed artists and communities work together.

✿ **DC (DANCE CREATORS)** is run by artistic directors of the African Cultural Exchange for young people and is based in Birmingham. DC is designed to respond to a generation bursting with creative ideas. The combination of popular dance styles, traditional African and Caribbean dance and music fused with experiences passed on through family connections, acts as a driving force – inspiring, educating and enabling young people to have a voice, to view things from another perspective, to translate their ideas into a visual language, to engage with digital technologies and to tackle social issues affecting their lives.

Dance as a part of a visual language uses physical bodies to create readable messages. Dance has given the young people involved new skills, the opportunity to look at different cultures and inter-culturalism and membership of a group which they feel they own. Working with African and Caribbean dance enables them to touch base with their cultural heritage but also to create a dance form that is Black British. Styles like hip hop and street dance are part of youth culture and are a vehicle for tackling issues that are relevant to them, their lives and their social backgrounds. DC have seen their work respected, appreciated and presented in a professional arena. A lot of time is spent discussing presentation, asking questions, looking at execution and dynamics, and trying to achieve quality in their work.

Information supplied by the Foundation for Community Dance.

Copies of the video Dancing Nation priced £15 (plus £1.50 p&p) can be obtained from Foundation for Community Dance, Cathedral Chambers, 2, Peacock Lane, Leicester LE1 5PX)

After leaving school at 14, IRENE ISON brought up three children as a single parent, earning a living as a fashion model and, after a horrific accident, a fortune-teller. She passed O levels in her 40s, A levels in her 50s and obtained a degree in Literary and Cultural Studies from Warwick University in her 60s.

In 1992 she won an Adult Learner of the Year Award. During this time she wrote short stories, poetry, plays and novels, many of which were published and performed. When her ex-husband and best friend became ill with cancer, she nursed him until he died. Her son then bought her a camera to help her get over the bereavement, and she became passionate about reportage photography.

Two years later at 67 she had gained five distinctions in a City and Guilds photography course at Tile Hill College in Coventry, had her photographs published in *Time Out* and the *London Evening Standard* and staged a number of exhibitions in her home town, when she was awarded the Licentiateship of the Royal Photographic Society of Great Britain.

In 1998 she spent six months walking around Coventry taking photographs of Coventry people, 30 of which were exhibited at the Herbert Art Gallery and Museum in Jordan Well. In 1999 she worked on a community photography project with single mothers from the Willenhall area of Coventry where she lives, aiming to show the regeneration of the estate through images of women and children. She said she wanted to show Willenhall not as an area going down but an area with a future.

Her exhibition in 2000, celebrating International Women's Day at the Museum of British Road Transport in Coventry, was entitled 'The Godiva Legacy', with 60 photographs capturing the extraordinary stories of ordinary women. She wanted to explore the idea that 'every woman displays courage – not just the high-profile ones'. Women in the photographs included a toilet cleaner, a *Big Issue* seller, a lollipop lady, a city bus driver, a single mother, a bowling group called Women with Balls, pupils and pensioners. The Pro-Vice Chancellor of the University of Warwick was also in the line-up, photographed on a Harley Davidson.

For the last few years Irene has also been teaching others about creative writing, quilt making and the history of women in photography. At present she is completing an MA in Photography at De Montfort University in Leicester.

'What have I given back in return for all these gifts?' she asks. ' I have taught community workshops in the local library for two years. I have created and photographed with local children a cookery book funded by the Government's Single Regeneration Budget. I have done the

IRENE ISON

photographs for a booklet about breast cancer for women with special educational needs. I am a parent supporter for parents of children with special educational needs. I work in the Oxfam Shop when I can. I am currently documenting the Coventry Community Carnival.'

Now she says, 'I want to get back to some writing. I want to write a play about Caitlin Thomas (Dylan's wife) which is in my head. I want to write the history of women in photography – buy a computer which won't let me down. Learn to play the guitar. Sing in a group, write some more poetry. Get on with a novel…'

SAD SATURDAY SAX

The spiteful wind smacked
bulky bags into shopper's legs. Hurled
furled leaves at marble pillars, snapped
bare branches from dead trees. Threw rubbish
at blind shop windows. Then suddenly stopped
to listen
as a sad Saturday saxophone sang
a slow song in the rain.

A melancholy melody, bringing nostalgic
smiles to neuralgic faces in the market. Eyes
of potatoes closed with ecstasy. Hearts of celery
melted clean away. Policemen tangoed with
villains, vandals dropped spray cans
to listen
as the haunting sound snaked around
the emptying evening streets.

Mothers stopped grumbling. Mumbling
pensioners did soft shoe shuffles. Muffled
children raised coloured mittens to capture
rapturous notes. Waiting bus queues swayed
stayed smiling, spirits lifting
to listen.
Souls responding to the longing
of the sad Saturday sax.

SECOND CITY SUNSET

In the city dusk
the fire glows.
Under the ringway bridge
lie sleepers, territories
Marked out carefully
with traffic cones.
A boulevard of benches
house the sad
and angry homeless,
who laugh briefly
at a weary old man's joke
he puffs a rolled cigarette.
Office workers clutch
samsonite briefcases
looking neither left nor right
as they run the gauntlet of
the bullring of the homeless.

Sparks snap and fly
from the flames
pushed into angry punishment
by a resentful boot.
During the day
they will scatter and beg.
But now at evening's approach
like starlings
who rest nestless
on the Town Hall ledges,
they sprawl, in the firelight sunset,
touched by Van Gogh,
cloth caps, punished faces.
Here's my Dad, my Grandad.
my daughter a slumbering
Pre-raphelite
in dirty plimsolls.

IRENE ON A
PHOTOSHOOT
CARL ISON

MERTON LIBRARY AND HERITAGE SERVICE has been awarded the prestigious *Libraries Change Lives* national award 'in recognition of excellence and good practice for library and information services in the local community'. Conferred by the Library Association in 2001 for outstanding work by libraries in the community, Merton overcame several strong contenders for the award to be the successful recipient.

Here are just some of the reasons why Merton Libraries caught the judges' eye:

✸ **REFUGEE RESOURCE COLLECTION AND SERVICE PROJECT**, a pioneering organisation, which aims to help asylum-seekers and refugees become self-sufficient and make a new life. Library staff regularly visit Asylum Welcome, a local drop-in centre where they issue books and other materials in a variety of identified minority ethnic languages. People attending the centre are taken to the nearest library to familiarise them with the kind of information that is available in the library. Staff also work with other groups of refugees and asylum-seekers elsewhere in the borough. These are people who are often longer established in this country but have specific information needs.

✸ **SPECIAL NEEDS GROUPS** Merton Libraries have taken a committed approach to tackling social exclusion through strategic objectives of community development, lifelong learning and economic regeneration. These objectives have been applied to services delivered by all libraries in the form of annual and five-year targets.

For example, goals have been set for outreach activities, registered users, library events/activities. Each library is expected to address these goals in the context of its local community profile and their needs. A special cost centre has been created for ethnic minority and outreach services with its own staff, budget and programme. This leads library services through an ambitious programme based on a number of relevant projects.

Special needs groups are those who do not traditionally use the library, or those who are marginalised by society. They include people who are disadvantaged because of their class, gender, sexuality, lack of adequate education, poor health, disability or who face exclusion through race, age (children and the elderly being vulnerable groups), poverty or a feeling that libraries cannot help or are not relevant.

Each library has compiled a community profile, originally based on census figures, but updated from local knowledge, issue statistics, local reference material, social services, education figures, partnership and community feedback, public consultation and word of mouth. These profiles are regularly updated and consulted so that groups with special needs can be identified, contact can be made and their needs can be assessed. Where appropriate, these details are passed on to the Equal Access cost centre so that initial contact can be established by staff at that cost centre.

⊛ TRAVELERS COLLECTION & SERVICE Travelers are recognised as one of the most severely educationally deprived sections of the community. In addition to the problems normally associated with lack of basic skills, Travelers frequently experience prejudice and discrimination from the settled community making it even more difficult for them to get services they need.

The Merton Libraries project involves a partnership with Sutton Libraries. Funded by the DCMS/Wolfson Public Libraries Challenge Fund. The project has created a resource collection – including books, jigsaws, toys, and adult basic skills materials – that can be used by Sutton and Merton Libraries and Sutton and Merton Traveler Education Service in their outreach work with Traveler communities. There are about 75 school-age Traveler children with several older and younger siblings and their extended families currently residing in Sutton and Merton.

The service is aimed at both adults and children. It also provides material for libraries in the two boroughs aimed at the non-Traveler population and includes a staff training programme provided by the Sutton and Merton Traveler Education Service.

The Mobile Library visits the Traveler site at Brickfield Road every other Friday. The children at the site who use the service would like to see more "Traveler" orientated books e.g. books on horses/fairs etc. Once the Traveler collection is catalogued, the project aims to satisfy this request.

⊙ **FESTIVAL OF EPHEMERAL ARTS** On Ephemeral Arts Day during One World Week eight different library sites provide a feast of multi-cultural activities for library users and members of the wider community. In his tribute to the libraries taking part, Iqbal Husain, Ethnic Arts and Community Development Officer, gives a flavour of the occasion: 'I was able to visit all libraries on the day and witness the various artists and participants at work. Highlights for me included two young women at Pollards Hill learning African mask-making and thoroughly enjoying the amusing descriptions the tutor employed to convey his craft; the library user at Raynes Park, who having arrived home and warming up her dumpling phoned the library to say how much she enjoyed the treat; the group of friends at Wimbledon Library learning Rangoli with colouring crayons; the young boy and his father taking part in the pottery workshop at Morden Library; the elderly lady who had been waiting at the Mobile Library stop in anticipation of the henna workshop; the Mayor of Merton at Mitcham library fascinated by what was on offer and keen to see similar multicultural work further promoted; the line of 'students' for Alpana at Donald Hope who were too busy to look up; and Ali Williams at West Barnes, thoroughly pleased with an eventful and fulfilling afternoon for her library users.'

⊙ **OTHER SERVICES** to the community include:

■ Regular visits to drop-in and community centres to issue material, join new readers, provide information and library publicity leaflets and assess needs. A complete list of outreach visits June 2000-February 2001 covers 13 pages.

■ Books in a variety of languages other than English including – Arabic, Bengali, Chinese, French, German, Gujarati, Hindi, Italian, Korean, Panjabi, Russian, Spanish, Tamil, Urdu. Film videos in languages including Hindi, Tamil, French, German, Italian, Spanish. African-Caribbean collections of black-interest books. South Asian collection in English

■ A Welcome pamphlet, translated into four languages so far, giving basic information pertinent to needs – homework clubs, language collections, open for learning computer centres within Merton libraries, English language classes, and so on.

■ Library use by special groups, initially through outreach, then through organised small group visits to libraries. Groups from North East Mitcham

Community Centre and Asylum Welcome have been taken by library staff to their nearest library for introductory visits.

■ Cultural, social and informational events e.g. Black History Month each October; One World Festival in February; drama presentations based on young refugees' experiences on arriving in Britain. Every library has been given targets to meet, including hosting a set number of community events each year. These are monitored to ensure that they happen.

■ Homework clubs. Extra funding is being sought for a homework helper specifically to support children whose first language is not English, as well as the existing help available from five homework clubs.

■ Area forums to consult with members of local minority communities. Meetings are held every two months. Ideas raised at these meetings are minuted, with an action list included at the end.

■ Current community partnerships include Asylum Welcome, Kent Libraries and Arts, London South West Chinese Community Association, Merton African Caribbean Organisation, Merton Asian Women's Association, North East Mitcham Community. Connections with publishers/booksellers who stock relevant material. These include New Beacon, Roy Yates, One World, Bookscan, Soma, Mantra, Milet, Africa Book Centre and the Refugee Council.

Information supplied by Shiraz Durrani, Merton Libraries
London Road, Morden, Surrey SM4 5DX.
Tel 020 8545 406   Email shiraz.durrani@merton.gov.uk

DANA CODOREAN BERCIU came to England in 1991 to rejoin her husband in exile, after nearly ten years of separation. She was born in Cluj in Transylvania and lived in a number of villages until her parents settled in Gherla, near Nicula, the main centre of Romanian painting on glass. After completing her art training in Bucharest she worked as an artist and teacher in Northern Transylvania from 1977.

It was impossible to portray religious subjects openly until the revolution in 1989 and the fall of the Ceaucescu regime, after which she began to develop her religious reverse painting on glass. She now works from her home in Camberwell using 'a resurrected movement of traditional art from Transylvania whose roots are steeped in mystery'.

Very little documentation exits about the origins of this technique which dates back to at least eighteenth century in Romania and which is also known in India and Ethiopia. Traditionally the technique of reverse painting on glass was used to convey the deep popular piety more commonly seen in orthodox icons.

Making use of their local glass industry, the village artists where Dana grew up chose this fragile medium in place of traditional wooden panels. The technique consists of rendering the main elements of composition on the back of the glass in thin black contours and superimposing, in reverse order, multiple layers of oil colours, in order to obtain an enamel-like effect, together with a generous use of gold leaf to emphasise significant areas of the painting.

For 40 years this art was gathered up and destroyed by the Ceausescu regime. Nowadays this very old technique is again under threat because it is only practised by a few remaining artists and crafts people and in one or two monasteries in Transylvania.

Dana studied the technique with a peasant artist at the small wooden monastery of Nicula and is now trying to revive an interest in the art form in Western Europe through a contemporary interpretation of the shapes and colours, whilst keeping the highly spiritual meaning alive. She says she wants to build bridges between Romanian and British culture – both through her stunning icon paintings on glass and her singing of old Romanian folk songs.

PAINTING ON GLASS OF ADAM AND EVE – BY DANA CODOREAN BERCIU

In 1995, Manchester City Council won the *Local Authority Race Award* – organised by the Commission for Racial Equality – for its outstanding services to refugee communities in Manchester. Both the **REFUGEE WORKING PARTY** and **MANCHESTER LIBRARIES & THEATRES DEPARTMENT** contributed to Manchester's winning entry, which showed how seriously the City Council takes its responsibilities to different refugee communities settled in the city and in encouraging these communities to participate in the life of the city. What follows is the background to this successful collaboration.

In September 1991 a cross-departmental working party was established by the City Council to address the needs of refugees from the Vietnamese and Somali communities. The terms of reference for the working party included:

- to review and co-ordinate the services provided for refugee in the city in the areas of Housing, Social Services, Education, Leisure (including libraries), and to recommend improvements.

- to produce an information pack (translated into the relevant languages) for refugees.

- to fully involve representatives of the refugee communities and appropriate non-statutory organisation in the work of the working party.

- to review the opportunities currently offered to refugees regarding employment within the City Council, and to propose action to improve matters.

- to investigate all avenues for procuring additional resources for refugees in Manchester.

Each participating department drew up an action plan to address issues which the communities had highlighted. For the Libraries and Theatres Department this included:

- co-ordinating the production of an information pack for refugees. The need for information on such vital matters as finding accommodation, providing heating, claiming for income support and sorting out schooling was top of the list from feedback with the community representatives. An information pack produced in both English/Vietnamese and English/Somali was widely distribute so that it could be used by both the refugees themselves and the agencies which were trying to help them.

■ the post of Advisor: Vietnamese Library Services was added to the establishment of the department.

The Refugee Working Party was never intended to go on forever. The aim was to ensure that refugee issues became an integral part of service planning. As such, it evolved into a smaller Officers Working Party Group which continued to research the needs of other refugee groups in Manchester.

The starting point for this was provided by the City Planning Office which produced a detailed "Social Survey of the Somali/Vietnamese communities in Manchester". Resources were not available to carry out such an in-depth exercise for other refugee groups. So the Officers Working Group set up a series of separate consultation meetings with representatives from Bosnian, Sudanese, Iraqi, Chilean and Vietnamese communities. Although the meetings were informal, they were structured around a set of questions which aimed to build a picture of needs of each group set in the context of their culture. The overriding aim of this exercise was for departmental action plans to reflect these needs where possible.

The library service was able to offer its meetings rooms and display space, and also offered to make community representatives aware of existing material in their language. Suggestions were also given by the refugees for books which could be added to the library stock.

In the case of the Vietnamese Library Service, a small collection of books was established in 1982, with help from local volunteers. Due to the popularity and usage of the collection and because of the extensive work done by the Refugee Working Party, Manchester Libraries recognised the importance of this service to the community and have made a real improvement in the library services to Vietnamese people. They created a special Vietnamese advisory post and added it to the establishment of the department. This post is based in North District, where the majority of Vietnamese people live, but it also has city-wide responsibility for developing the service, as well as promoting awareness of Vietnamese culture.

Crumpsall Library is at last gaining national attention for its services for the Vietnamese community. It now has the largest collection in the country of:

- Vietnamese books
- Music cassettes & CDs
- BBC tapes
- Videos & Video-CDs
- Leaflets & periodicals
- Displays at libraries and community venues to promote services
- Spoken-word
- Vietnamese word-processing, CD-ROMs and Internet Services
- Dual-language books

The library has also organised events for the community such as:

- new stock launches organised on a yearly basis, including old stock sales
- dual-language story telling and cultural awareness sessions to school children and staff both in schools and in libraries – this greatly benefits the local children in the community.
- author talk events
- exhibitions relevant to local communities

Ongoing work with community groups include:

- producing a newsletter with Manchester Vietnamese Community Association.
- work with the Vietnamese Cultural Group to run Mother Tongue classes for children at Abraham Moss Centre on Saturdays.
- helping to organise celebrations for the Vietnamese Moon festival and New Year – the most important festivals in the Vietnamese calendar.

Information supplied by Hoi Dong: The Vietnamese Library Support Network, Crumpsall Library, Abraham Moss Centre Crescent Road, Crumpsall, Manchester M8 5UF Tel: 0161 721 4555 Fax: 0161 721 4927 Email: hoidong@libraries.manchester.gov.uk

Cities like London are crammed full of people with no connection to each other. The National Trust's **LONDON LINKS** project, funded by the Regional Arts Lottery Programme, emerged from investigating ways of breaking down feelings of isolation and exclusion as part of moves to widen access to Trust sites for local people living near to the sites. With the help of professional artists, local community groups created their own responses to four different National Trust places through a variety of art forms, including printing, puppetry, photography and storytelling.

Ham House near Richmond – this project worked with children whose families are refugees or asylum seekers, from countries including Kosovo, Afghanistan, Somalia and Iran.

No 2 Willow Road in Hampstead – the stimulus for users of Camden and Islington Mental health NHS Trust. Guided by an artist experienced in working with people with mental health problems, and mental health workers from the Royal Free Hospital, the group developed creative responses to the house and its unique collection of modern art, through painting and drawing.

Sutton House in Hackney – a project with three groups of homeless people, who explored the concept of 'home' and what it means to different people. The group members were keen to find ways of interpreting the story of the house when it was used as a squat in the 1980s, rather than the more usual stories of this Tudor merchant's house.

Morden Hall Park in an urban area of South West London, Pillar Box – a parent and toddler group from the local housing estate chose to work with a storyteller and an illustrator. The children and their parents produced large illustrated books based on stories they created about the creatures of the park which they discovered in this 'green oasis'.

London Links culminated in a sharing of this work at Sutton House in Hackney. Participants came with their families and friends and enjoyed the puppet shows, poems and music, and photographs, pictures and collages on display. London Links will continue next year with three more properties and some different community groups who will join in the activities.

All of the participants enjoyed being involved in the project. They variously described it as a 'rare', 'unique' and 'wonderful' opportunity, a 'positive, rewarding experience'. One said the project meant 'being able to forget I was unwell'. 'Discernable gains in self-esteem and self-confidence' were made by mixing with the National Trust staff and the artists, who showed them that 'art is not for others'. Comments included, 'I feel like a celebrity, it's great. I don't want it to be over'. 'It's different from the normal things I get involved in – I've enjoyed what I've seen and the prints I've produced. I hope they show what it's really like to live in a hostel.' Staff and volunteers talked about their own sense of job satisfaction and personal development. All the artists were equally pleased with the quality of the work produced. They commented, 'very professional and creative', 'a brave process of exploration of new ideas and techniques, hard work and concentration, together with a sensitive appreciation and response to the collection.'

The project gave the sites a great opportunity to develop their links with the local communitiy and encouraged them to further develop their community education and outreach strategies.

Information supplied by Laura Hetherington, Head of Education and Interpretation, and Polly Andrews, Education Projects Officer, The National Trust

SUTTON HOUSE
WRITERS' GROUP

NATIONAL TRUST
PHOTOGRAPHIC LIBRARY
/ DAVID LEVENSON

At consultation meetings during the 1996 Festival of Sea and the 1997 Community Festival in Bristol it became clear that members of black community groups felt that the city did not properly acknowledge its role in slavery. In 1998 Bristol Museums Service held an open meeting with different groups to talk about how they would like to see slavery presented and acknowledged. An action group was formed of councillors, members of the black community, museum officers and academics, to look at how a story of Bristol's part in the slave trade could be told historically and accurately. Using a process of ongoing consultation and discussion, three different projects were developed. The Georgian House Museum and some of its displays were reinterpreted in the light of fresh information about how the building and most of its contents had been bought using money earned from the slave trade and slave-produced commodities. Bristol Museums and Art Gallery produced a Slave Trade Trail and booklet to use around central Bristol, showing all the buildings and institutions that were created by the slave trade and slave produced commodities. Bristol Museums and Art Gallery then staged a temporary exhibition about the Transatlantic Slave Trade and its effects on people's lives – both slaves and people in Bristol – interpreted from an African perspective. The exhibition has now become permanent at the Bristol Industrial Museum.

Community consultation helped produce a more balanced exhibition with different and African perspectives included. Part of it looks at African cultures before the slave trade, another represents black people's struggle and the Abolition Movement, whilst the last shows visitors the legacies slavery has left today and asks for their own response. Another important aspect is to humanise the story, by looking at the individual people involved.

Consultation meetings were also held with museum workers, espressing concern about the exhibition. Two training sessions were held there, led by a community activist and the Director of Bristol Race Equality Council. The staff were involved in discussions, cultural awareness training and a gallery tour. The museum also decided to have interpreters from the African community answer visitors' questions about the exhibition and provide an African perspective to white visitors.

This project demonstrates courageous and responsive work, confronting difficult issues with commitment and sensitivity.

For further details contact Bristol City Museum and Art Gallery and see 'Museums and Social Inclusion: The GLAMM Report' (2000)

The Triangular Trade

The slave trade was part of a 'triangular' trading network between Britain, West Africa and the Caribbean, together with British colonies in North America.

The transatlantic slave trade was begun by the Portuguese in the 15th century. By the 18th century Britain had become one of the most important slave-trading nations in the world with Bristol at the forefront.

Bristol

Slave-produced commodities (sugar, rum, tobacco, cotton, cocoa and coffee) shipped to Bristol for refining and processing, and then sold on.

America and the Caribbean

Atlantic Ocean

Manufactured goods from Bristol (guns, textiles, alcohol and metalware) shipped to West Africa and sold or exchanged for human beings.

The 'middle passage'. Enslaved Africans shipped and sold to supply labour for British plantation in the Caribbean and colonies in North America.

STANSFIELD & Cᵒˢ
Super Fine Tobacco,
Caftle-Street BRISTOL.

SOURCE H
Advertisement from Stansfield & Co, tobacconists.

Opposition to the slave trade gained momentum during the late 18th century. The trade was abolished in British territories in 1807, but the slaves themselves were not granted full freedom until 1838.

West Africa

PUBLISHED BY BRISTOL MUSEUMS

ROSA CHIRICO
GHOST — ONE
GHOSTLY PHOT
STORY, USING
ROOM SETTING
THE CECIL HIG(
ART GALLERY I
BEDFORD, VIC1
COSTUMES AN
WONDERS OF
PHOTOGRAPHY
OF THE SIXTY
TONGUES OF
BEDFORD PRO

Bread and Roses

8

REPRISE AND RECOMMENDATIONS

The starting point for this exploration into art and culture and lifelong learning was the recognition that 'hearts starve as well as bodies' and that in order to assuage two different kinds of hunger, citizens in a just society are entitled to both bread and roses. The expression of pleasure, consuming passion, purpose and creativity through arts and culture, as a way of enhancing the quality of people's lives, cannot be underestimated. The current commitment to lifelong learning seems to recognise this, although, as we have seen, economic priorities effectively distort the balance between the vocational, the personal, the social and the creative dimensions of learning. At a time when the interests of the state and the economy have focused on securing labour market skills and qualifications at the expense of liberal and popular education, it is important to remember that such provision is critically important to resourcing cultural renewal, democratic participation and active citizenship. So long as the emphasis is on human capital, the intellectual and political significance of social and cultural capital remains neglected. For a well-informed, socially-just and politically-engaged society, we need the full range of learning opportunities that contribute to the well-being of all citizens, in provision that is available not simply to those who are employed or employable, but to everyone.

In addition, the emphasis on labour market skills underestimates the extent to which leisure activities and consumption have become increasingly significant as a source of identity and pleasure in people's lives, in the context of an ageing and increasingly diverse population. As in the rest of Europe, lower birth rates and increased longevity in Britain mean that by 2010 as many as 40 per cent of the population in Western and Northern Europe will be in the age group between 45 and 65. This not only creates a huge potential for participation in learning and cultural activity but it also requires a policy commitment which recognises that the lives of middle-aged and older people are important and should be meaningful.

Debates about access and about widening participation in adult learning are not new but they are still unresolved. What is provided 'still benefits too narrow a segment of the population. Whereas the overall numbers of adult participants in organised learning have grown over the last decade, their social composition has remained stubbornly resistant to change'.[84] Those who regularly participate in arts and cultural activities are not vastly different in terms of class and ethnic background from those who take part in adult learning. Those who are poorest, least well-educated, not economically active, most marginalised, and whose cultural identities are hardest to negotiate in a predominantly white and middle-class cultural ambience, are least likely to believe that such activities have anything to do with them.

Too frequently the tendency remains to attribute non-participation in learning to individual deficiencies or lack of motivation rather than to the failure of the education system to be relevant or attractive to the majority of the adult population. Arts and cultural organisations should appear to be more conducive, not least because they are frequently associated with entertainment and the pursuit of pleasure. But they also carry historic connotations of social exclusivity and cultural elitism which act as barriers to those whose background and education have not provided them with the 'right' cultural capital to deal with what are effectively white and middle-class activities. Those who do gain access usually find, as with education, that inequalities of class, race and gender are still more important than individual talent or commitment when it comes to feeling at home. McGivney puts it like this:

> It is an indication of our ambivalence towards people who are educationally and socially-disadvantaged, that when they do engage successfully in formal learning and aspire to higher qualification levels, their incursion into a world so long and so firmly dominated by the middle-classes is greeted with widespread alarm. Having previously been held responsible for their lack of educational participation and progress, new groups who enter further and higher education by 'non-standard' routes are blamed for lowering and devaluing the standards. This is like inviting people to a private club but when they get there, informing them it is for members only. In the first year of the new millennium, there is still a 'class' ceiling in our education and training system that is waiting to be smashed.[85]

It is not surprising that widening participation in arts and cultural activities face similar assumptions: which is why arguments for change need to start from a different position.

CULTURAL RENEWAL

One possible place is that identified by Raymond Williams in his insistence that 'culture is ordinary' and that it makes no sense 'to produce the extraordinary fussiness, this extraordinary decision to call certain things culture and then separate them, as with a park wall, from ordinary people and ordinary work'.[86] Artistic culture and culture as a way of life are mutually dependent.

It is not the case that culture comprises a fixed entity that can be commonly agreed upon, easily identified and, before you know where you are, displayed in a museum or stored in a library. The point about culture is that it is made through human interaction and it changes. Everyone has a part to play in contributing to the activity of defining what culture means – in both senses of the term. The nature and quality of a shared culture – including the influential characteristics of race, class, age and gender, for example – are not pre-determined; they are learned. But they are also lived, experimented-with and changed in the process of pushing up against their established limitations. These are social negotiations that involve conflict, restriction and power, but also co-operation, resilience and desire. They are the negotiations that create the stuff of human existence. They are also the wellspring out of which the real force of art originates.

The other critical point about culture – again, in both senses of the term – is that what is not present is essential to making sense of what is possible in order for cultures to grow and change. From this position, culture – like democracy – is always still to come and requires the active involvement of everyone in determining how to go about it and what might be possible. For Williams the urgent concern is to interconnect art and culture, in the certainty that

> In many respects these arts will be changed…if we understand cultural growth…we should clear the channels to let all the offerings be made, taking care to give the difficult full space, the

original full time, so that there is a real growth and not just another confirmation of the old rules.[87]

In Richard Hoggart's words:

> A would-be civilised democracy will not abuse culture for immediate political ends, nor impose its own pre-determined definitions of culture on its people. It will be open, democratic, not bullying, not necessarily all-things-to-all-men-or-women. It will offer perspectives on the better and the best; its citizens will be free to be both inside and outside their own cultural overcoats.[88]

What this argument means for us is that art and culture should reflect culture and society in all its complexity and diversity. What is regarded as 'the best that has been thought and said' – as well as created or performed – should be available to everyone, not simply a privileged few, as a right of cultural democracy. Equal access to the best of culture is worth fighting for, in the same way as social and economic equality are worth fighting for. In the process, we should understand that what is thought by some to be 'the best' will inevitably change, to reflect what has not previously been present, and what is still to be imagined.

This obviously has implications for educational provision. If we accept the substance of the argument, it means that educational provision should:

■ focus on learners – systems concerned with outreach, access and support should start and proceed in relation to the needs and to the material and cultural circumstances of learners, rather than the needs and requirements of systems.

■ focus on the curriculum – how does the knowledge which is being taught connect to the lived experience of the learners? Does it give time to the difficult? Does it make space for the different? Does it welcome new and alternative knowledge? Does it provide for dissent and agreement? Does it help to cultivate the narrative imagination?

■ focus on pedagogy – dialogue and inter-active teaching methods – concerned to develop creativity, problem-solving, critical thinking and tolerant and reflective attitudes – are much more likely to enhance learning than transmission or facilitation.

SOCIAL EXCLUSION

A second position is the one that starts from the consequences of living in a society in which poverty and inequality affects the lives of millions of people.

In response to this situation, political radicals usually begin by analysing the economic and structural basis of social inequality and emphasising the need for social and political changes to redistribute wealth, resources and power to create a more equal and socially just society. Rahman and his colleagues acknowledge that the present Government has introduced a wide range of initiatives to tackle the problems of poverty and social exclusion but say it is not yet clear whether the initiatives are collectively sufficient to address the scale and depth of the problems over time, or how successful they will be in helping the more disadvantaged to catch up – or at least keep up – with the rest of society.[89]

In his discussion of globalisation, lifelong learning and culture, Colin Griffin warns against focussing on learning (and the same could be said of arts and culture) as an object of cultural engineering and of retreating from education policies in favour of strategies. According to Griffin, 'there is a considerable difference between policy and strategy in respect of the achievement of policy goals. Strategies such as the University for Industry, or voucher schemes, or tax breaks, remain incentives for individuals to take responsibility for their own learning, rather than policies for the redistribution of educational opportunity. (Trying) to change people's attitudes and values towards self-development may not have any effect on the deep and growing structural inequalities in society and are unlikely to deal effectively with social inequality'[90]. This is rather the same conclusion reached by Gilbert and colleagues in their study of museums and social inclusion. Whilst they found a lot of enthusiasm among policy makers in relation to social inclusion, they had to conclude that 'the ability of museums and galleries to socially engineer society, while an attractive idea to many museum workers, cannot at present be demonstrated'.[91] It is just possible, however, that in the current political climate, policy and strategy are seen to be the same thing. But if we allow them to be so, it could mean that the incapacity or unwillingness of the state to deliver social objectives such as social inclusion, citizenship and equality becomes disguised by a wide range of incentives for individuals to improve themselves, and to make themselves more employable and socially included through learning. Not only does this enable us to hold those self-same individuals responsible if they don't succeed, rather than the structural and economic forces and trends over which they have no control, but it opens the flood gates to Ritzer's nightmare scenario of standardisation in production and consumption through the application of uniform criteria of efficiency, measurement, predictability and control.[92] The proliferation of initiatives and strategies inevitably requires the proliferation of bureaucratic structures of control and accountability – in relation to funding, accreditation, quality assurance and inspection regimes, for example. Whilst I do not doubt the sincerity of those who seek to widen participation and to combat social exclusion in arts, culture and lifelong learning systems, it is to be hoped that such aspirations are not stifled by the bureaucratic forms upon which they so frequently rely. It is heartening in this context that Tessa Blackstone intends to argue for 'minimum bureaucracy, maximum money'.

If we accept the substance of this argument it means that:

- the creation of a socially more inclusive society depends on Governments being prepared to define options that envisage a multi-racial and socially just society, in ways that commit serious public spending to public services and that implement resource redistribution, including the redistribution of educational and cultural resources .

- social engineering cannot be achieved without the social and economic redistribution of resources

- short-term strategies and initiatives that rely on incentives to individuals to modify and change their behaviour in line with dominant (white, middle-class) norms are unlikely to deal effectively with deep structural and social inequalities. Money spent on bureaucratic rationalisation to administer and support systems of accountability and control in lifelong learning and the arts comes at the expense of actual learning and actual participation. Money spent on bureaucracy is in danger of funding the management of social exclusion rather than the alleviation of poverty.

The liberal stance, on the other hand, takes social inequality for granted, or at least, as being unlikely to change significantly. It then seeks to alleviate the worst excesses of social injustices by opening up access to resources and increasing participation in activities that might ameliorate people's lives or help them to shift their position. Such a stance often involves a great deal of energy and a determination to promote institutional change.

> If social inclusion means anything, it means actively seeking out and removing barriers, and acknowledging that people, who have been left out for generations, need additional support in a whole variety of ways to enable them to exercise their right to participate in many of the facilities that the better-off and better-educated take for granted.[93]

This approach, when it is supported by committed policy-makers, providers and enthusiastic practitioners, argues for openness of access, the recognition and celebration of diversity, the power of learning and the arts to improve the quality of people's lives. Much is made of raising confidence and self-esteem and of the recognition that success can breed success. Role models, champions, ambassadors and mentors all have a role to play in spreading the word and encouraging their peers and others like themselves to get involved. Taster sessions, first-rung provision and personal achievement can all help to break down barriers to participation and heighten expectations. Heightened confidence leads to heightened awareness and heightened pressure for more and better provision. In this kind of context, policy-makers and providers are on the look-out for evidence of what works, how to do it and how to spread it around. Developments derive from a project culture, which at best illuminates good practice but which is fraught with all the well-known frustrations and restraints associated with short-term funding and continuous, competitive bidding.

In the hands of more cynical and/or less reflexive professionals, the pursuit of projects and initiatives can so easily become pragmatic and concerned with doing 'just enough' to comply with what is required to supply outcomes and fulfil funding obligations, so that the 'real body of work' can continue undisturbed.

The evidence from the reports and their recommendations discussed earlier suggests that whilst considerable enthusiasm and examples of good practice do exist, there is still a long way to go when it comes to strategic leadership, political and social understanding of the issues, inter-agency collaboration and adequate core funding directed towards building and sustaining socially inclusive policies.

According to this view, arguments for institutional change matter because there are powerful benefits to be gained by currently excluded groups, actual and potential learners and people using cultural resources if education and the culture sector develop closer links. This will mean:

- recognising that since the widening participation dynamic is common to both lifelong learning and culture – it makes sense to collaborate.

- building in closer links and more liaison between the Department for Education and Skills, the Department of Culture, Media and Sport and the Learning and Skills Council.

- ensuring that future funding for national policy initiatives concerned with widening participation and neighbourhood renewal, for example, contain explicit provision for arts and cultural activities.

So far as cultural organisations are concerned, it means:

- working more closely, and in collaboration, with other domains in the culture sector, as well as other social, educational and cultural organisations in public and civil society

- recognising that educators in cultural organisations can help people with guidance, can help to structure their learning and can link them to other existing resources.

- recognising that artists in residence – in educational and community organisations of various kinds – make the cultural dimensions of learning and social activity more visible.

- putting equal opportunities at the centre of the work rather than adding-on specific provision at the margins

- ensuring that regular consultation, dialogue and collaboration occurs with representatives of excluded groups and taking outreach seriously

- accepting that many of the conventions and rituals of arts and cultural settings may need to be modified and diversified in order to welcome new participants

- recognising that information-giving should respond to participants with different levels of education and different amounts of prior knowledge

- re-defining research and development in order that staff are as informed and rigorous about participants as they are about their exhibits, collections, and performances.

- developing shared staff training/development opportunities to foster collaborative practices across boundaries

IN CONCLUSION

Although initiatives, projects and strategies remain the reality in present political and economic circumstances, what is palpably missing from their momentum is the compelling force of a shared imagining of change, and a sense of collective hope. The radical language of art, education, imagination and creativity frequently collapses into pragmatism and shallowness. Human needs, unfulfilled desires, the passion for justice, the possibility of connection and social transformation are translated into objects and commodities. Participants are marked out as customers and consumers. The poor and the variously excluded become targets to be ticked-off. In an audit culture, we operate as if only those things which can be counted – count.

To go further from what is a relatively limited obligation to offer physical access to previously excluded groups, to also providing cultural, emotional and intellectual access to the meaning, the understanding and the creation of art and culture requires fundamental changes to take place in the general assumptions and conventions of arts and cultural organisations. In this respect, the broadcast media have a key role to play in media literacy, cultural democracy and aesthetics and in making these accessible to everyone. This is not an argument for dumbing-down but for democratising learning and about starting not from where arts and cultural institutions think is 'here' but with people. And this takes time.

What we need is much less in the way of targeting the socially excluded via short-term initiatives that usually serve institutional funding interests and much more in the way of sustained alliances between government, education and cultural workers and ordinary people. These should be alliances that are built on equality and respect, and the will to deal with social, educational and cultural issues together, in ways that are challenging, principled, properly resourced, redistributive and which welcome much greater dialogue between all those of us involved.

Coming together with others to define common, unfulfilled desires and needs, and to identify the forces that frustrate them, can be a powerful tonic for the imagination. The sense of common purpose and intention to make a difference is the stuff of social transformation – both in learning and in art. In those words, images and symbols, whereby we recognise ourselves, and name our condition in the company of others – in ways that celebrate difference, generate understanding and encourage activity – lies the possibility, not simply of resistance to being ill-served, but of the energy and imagination to create something better.

---

[84] V McGivney (2001) *Fixing or Changing the Pattern? Reflections on Widening Participation in Learning,* Leicester: NIACE

[85] V McGivney (2001) 'Informal learning and bridging the class divide in educational participation', in *Rising East*, Vol 4, Number 2, pp38-52

[86] R Williams (1958) *op cit*

[87] *ibid*

[88] R Hoggart (2001) *op cit*

[89] M Rahman, G Palmer and Kenway (2001) *Monitoring Poverty and Social Exclusion*, Joseph Rowntree Foundation.

[90] C Griffin (2001) ' Lifelong Learning and Culture' in *International Yearbook of Adult Education*, 28/29, Bohlau Verlag: Köln

[91] E Gilbert *et al* (2001) *The Contribution of Museums to the Inclusive Community: An Exploratory Study*. For further details of this research and future developments, please contact Andrew Newman, Department of Archaeology, University of Newcastle upon Tyne

[92] G Ritzer (1992) *The McDonaldisation of Society*, Thousand Oaks: Pine Forge

[93] M O'Neill (2001) *op cit*